Nila Banton Smith

LEVEL C

Be a Better Reader

BASIC SKILLS EDITION

Prentice-Hall, Inc., Englewood Cliffs, N. J.

PRONUNCIATION KEY

Symbol	Key Word	Symbol	Key Word	Symbol	Key Word
a	act, lap	u	up, nut	n	nap, noon
ā	age, late	ū	use, few	p	play, top
ã	dare, hair	ũr	fur, learn	r	ran, steer
ä	star, father	ə	a in along	s	sit, yes
e	end, met		e in moment	t	tip, hat
ē	see, even		i in modify	v	very, wave
ê	here, clear		o in protect	w	wide, always
ẽr	over, under		u in circus	y	yellow, onion
i	hit, is	b	big, job	z	zebra, freeze
ī	ice, mile	d	do, red	ch	chill, reach
o	dot, plot	f	fair, if	sh	sharp, crash
ō	no, open	g	go, dig	th	three, both
ô	corn, border	h	head, behave	ŦH	then, breathe
oo	book, put	j	joke, bridge	zh	treasure
o͞o	move, school	k	king, kick	ŋ	bring, think
oi	foil, boy	l	light, bell	′	heavy accent (stress)
ou	out, crowd	m	meet, him	′	light accent (stress)

Acknowledgments:
Unit 1 — [1]Adapted from Vol. 12, *Childcraft — The How and Why Library.* © 1971 Field Enterprises Educational Corporation. *Unit 4* — [2]From *Your Career In Unusual Occupations,* by Walter Harter. © 1971, by Walter Harter. Reprint permission from David McKay, publishers. [3]"Alone on an Island" adapted from "The Hot-Tempered Boy" by Murray T. Pringle from STORY PARADE copyright 1952 by Story Parade, Inc. Adapted by permission of Western Publishing Company, Inc. *Unit 5* — [4]Copyright © 1966 HIGHLIGHTS FOR CHILDREN, INC., Columbus, Ohio. *Unit 6* — [5]Adapted from Vol. 13, *Childcraft — The How and Why Library.* © 1971 Field Enterprises Educational Corporation.

Art Credits:

Al Lorenz: pages 4, 7, 36, 39, 64, 69, 71, 92, 94, 123, 125, 155, 157, 183, 185.

Emil Peter Marcionetti: pages 8, 9, 21, 25, 29, 30, 31, 32, 40, 72, 88, 114, 116, 118, 120, 141, 178, 180, 199, 200, 202.

Don + Ann Crews: pages 14, 15, 18, 20, 28, 48, 52, 53, 58, 60, 61, 62, 79, 81, 82, 86, 117, 119, 136, 137, 139, 151, 193, 194, 196, 197, 201.

Photographic Credits:
pages 1 — Air France Photo; 13 — top right: Culver Pictures; 35 — Japan National Tourist Organization; 45 — Library of Congress; 46 — left: Culver Pictures; right: Art Institute of Chicago; 55 — New York Public Library Picture Collection; 57 — New York Public Library Picture Collection; 59 — Woodrow Paster/Photo Researchers; 67 — United Nations; 73 — Gunter R. Reitz/De Wys; 74 — De Wys; 76 — United Nations; 77 — Jim Theologos; 90 — Courtesy Bermuda News Bureau; 99 — Pat Collins/Sea Library; 100 — Jim Theologos; 102 — John H. Gerard/Photo Researchers; 103 — top, right: Jim Theologos; left: Gordon Smith/Photo Researchers; bottom, left: Robert Hermes/Photo Researchers; right: John H. Gerard/Photo Researchers; 104 — top, left: Russ Kinne/

(continued on page iv.)

Be a Better Reader, Level C, Basic Skills Edition
Nila Banton Smith

Printed in the United States of America

10 9 8

ISBN 0-13-074112-4

Prentice-Hall International, Inc.
London

Prentice-Hall of Australia, Pty. Ltd.,
Sydney

Prentice-Hall of Canada, Ltd.,
Toronto

Prentice-Hall of India Private Ltd.,
New Delhi

Prentice-Hall of Japan, Inc.,
Tokyo

Designed by Madeline Bastis & Friends

TABLE OF CONTENTS

(continued from page ii.)
W. Putney/Photo Stock Library; 126 — top: United Press International; bottom: London Times; 128 — Larry Reeve/Photo Stock Library; 130 — United Nations; 131 — Chapelle/ Monkmeyer; 133 — New York Public Library Picture Collection; 134 — left: Culver Pictures; center and right: New York Public Library Picture Collection: 152 — Everett C. Johnson/De Wys; 153 — Lew Merrim/Monkmeyer; 160 — De Wys; 163 — top: Photo Researchers; right: Walter Dawn/ Photo Researchers; bottom, left: Carleton Ray/Photo Researchers; right: Douglas

Marlo/Photo Researchers; 110 — New York Public Library Picture Collection; 121 — top: United Nations; bottom: Thomas Jim Cron/Monkmeyer; bottom: De Wys; 165 — top: Hugh Rogers/Monkmeyer; bottom: Monkmeyer; 166 — De Wys; 167 — Sydlow/Monkmeyer; 168 — Caravallo/Monkmeyer; 171 — De Wys; 181 — Sybil Shackman/Monkmeyer; 187 — Jim Theologos; 190 — UNIVAC, Division of Sperry Rand Corporation; 192 — Sybil Shackman/Monkmeyer; 193 — Sybil Shackman/Monkmeyer; 195 — Thomas W. Putney/Photo Stock Library; 198 — P. Vannucci/De Wys.

1

Challenges
from the Sky

HOW TO READ
LITERATURE

Written for this book
by Sheila L. Burns.

When we see or hear or read a good story, we usually want to tell it to somebody else. People everywhere enjoy good stories. They like to hear them, and they like to tell them. In places where there are no schools, no radio, and no TV, people value good storytellers. They gather around a storyteller and listen for hours — even when they have heard the same stories many times before. We, too, will hurry through our tasks so that we can watch TV — our favorite storyteller.

Why do people like stories so much? There seem to be many reasons. One reason is that through our imaginations we can live someone else's life for a while. We can be a doctor who is working to save a life, or a racing car driver, or a spy on the run. We can take on another person's worries and hopes, and escape from our own for a time.

Another reason stories are popular is that we learn many things from them. We learn why some people act as they do. We find out about life in other places and other times. We can travel into the past or the future, to another planet or some other place we may never see in real life.

We also share many different feelings with the persons in a story. People sitting around a campfire on a dark night actually enjoy being frightened by a ghost story. People who cried through most of a movie put away their wet handkerchiefs happily and claim that they had a very good time. We even joke about giving movies a rating of "one handkerchief" or "two handkerchiefs" instead of one or two stars.

Practically everyone has heard this about a story: "I didn't like the ending." Sometimes people don't like an ending because it is sad. At other times, they don't like it because it does not make sense. The ending may not fit the rest of the story. In this case, people may say that a story is "bad."

What makes a story "good"? In this unit, we shall explore that question. A good storyteller, like a good carpenter or chef, is a skilled worker. He or she has tools and materials and a way of fashioning a product which can be examined and understood.

There are all kinds of stories, and one person may not like all kinds. Stories can be funny or sad, full of action or quiet, as long as a book or as short as one page. A story can have many people in it, or one, or none. Some stories are true; others are made up.

Even though stories vary a great deal, in some ways they are alike. A carpenter, for instance, could make tables in a hundred different styles. Yet each table would be like the others in at least some ways. So, too, we can see some of the same elements in every story.

Some of the elements you will find in nearly every story are these:

1. *plot*—the events that happen in the story
2. *characters*—the persons in the story
3. *setting*—the time of the story and the place where it occurs
4. *conflict*—a problem faced in the story
5. *theme*—the main idea you take away from the story.

In this unit, we shall be looking most closely at the plot of a story. In other parts of this book, you will examine the other elements.

The plot of a story is what happens. It is a series of events. The events can be actions you can see, such as driving, sewing, running, talking, crying, fighting. The events can also be actions you would not know about except for the story. These are the private thoughts of a person, his or her feelings, decisions, schemes, and dreads which may not be shared with anyone but the reader. These invisible actions can be important to our understanding. They explain all the actions that we can see.

Every story has a beginning, middle, and end. It is important to keep the events of a story in the right order. A storyteller may start off with one event, then later tell you of something that happened before that. The first thing you hear is not always the first thing that happened.

In "The Wrong Angle," look carefully at the plot of the story. Notice what events happened before the story began. The story makes better sense if you put the events in the right order in your mind.

You will enjoy the story more if you know all the words. Before you read, study the word helps at the bottom of the page. Work out the pronunciation and think about the meaning. Then when you see the word in the story, you will know what it means.

The whole world cheered when our astronauts conquered space. They are modern heroes daring to go into the unknown. Another kind of heroism, though, is that shown by the astronauts' families. They had to stand by quietly and watch while a father or husband risked his life. Knowing the risks, they watched every move on TV. How do you suppose they felt, when a member of their family came within a hair's-breadth of lonely death in the sky? This story will tell you how it was for the family of Malcolm Scott Carpenter. On May 24, 1962, his family watched while he became the second American to orbit the earth.

The Wrong Angle

Written by René Carpenter.[1]

Jay dropped to the floor and sprawled out on his stomach with his legs straight out behind him. The points of his elbows dug into the rug and he cupped his chin in his hands. He stared at the television screen. The TV announcer's voice droned on and on, telling about the space flight that was now nearly completed.

Jay listened to the voice without paying attention. He was thinking about the man who was in the space capsule that was orbiting the earth. That man was his dad.

[1]Numbered footnote references will be found on page ii.

capsule (kap's'l), a compartment for the astronauts in a spaceship

booster (boos'tẽr), a device which helps increase power

re-entry (rē en'trē), coming back into the earth's atmosphere

retrorocket (ret'rō rok'it), a small rocket which produces a thrust opposite to a spacecraft's direction in order to slow speed

4

Jay looked around the room. His mother's eyes were glued to the screen. She seemed to have forgotten that there was anyone else in the room with her. Jay's big brother Scotty was sitting on a footstool next to his mother. Scotty was restless. He kept fidgeting. Jay's two little sisters, Candy and Krissie, seemed bored. Candy was half asleep, almost falling off her footstool. Krissie was staring at the wall above the TV set. Her eyes were opened wide and her mouth drooped as if she were off in some daydream world. Her legs dangled over the edge of her chair and swung slowly back and forth.

The room was quiet except for the sounds coming from the TV set. Much of the excitement and eagerness they had all felt that morning had passed. Now there was not much to do but to watch and wait as the hours crawled by. Jay thought back to early that morning, when the rocket carrying his father had blasted off from Cape Canaveral. It had been the most thrilling moment of Jay's life. Shortly before blastoff his father had phoned from the capsule to tell them of the preparations. The sounds of the booster below him carried over the telephone. After the phone call, the family had returned to the TV set as the countdown neared its end.

At the count of zero they had watched the huge rocket ship hang suspended over the launching pad and then start to rise slowly into the air. They all raced outside the beach-house to watch the rocket, which was only a few miles away, lift out of the ground fog and soar up and up into the sky. Then they had rushed back into the house again to watch the rocket being tracked on a special telescope lens until it disappeared from the TV screen.

Jay had been more excited than he had ever been before. For a long while he had listened to all the reports that came in. He could even hear his father's voice, although it was a faraway voice, punctuated with static—a voice that didn't sound like his father's at all.

Their father had given both boys a copy of his flight plan so that they would know what he was doing throughout the flight. He would be making nearly forty experiments and observations, and the family was listening eagerly for the reports. He would photograph the colors of sunrise and sunset, and he would launch a balloon from the capsule to see whether it would drag behind or follow alongside the capsule.

With his copy of the flight plan, Jay knew when each experiment would take place. He imagined his father trying to eat solid foods in the weightlessness of space. He wondered what would happen to a flask of liquid when there was no up or down. Jay tried to picture what his father saw, looking down at the earth's cloud formations from outer space. And Jay imagined himself looking for the strange particles of light that Colonel Glenn, another astronaut, had described as looking like fireflies.

Jay listened closely to the reports as they came in. Sometimes the TV announcer gave the information, and sometimes Jay could hear his father's voice making the reports. As the morning wore on, Jay learned that the balloon experiment had been spoiled when the balloon had filled up only part way. He laughed when he found out that the solid food had crumbled and floated around the capsule when his dad had tried to eat. And then Jay discovered that his dad had spotted the strange particles of light, which he described as looking like snowflakes.

The news of these and the other experiments had held Jay's attention for most of the morning. But after a while the children had grown restless. Jay and Scotty had started wrestling and rolling across the floor. But their mother had stopped them. Instead, she had them do push-ups. And later she had given them lunch, made them do the dishes, and sent them out to swim on the beach.

Now the morning was gone and soon their father would be coming back down to earth. That was the most dangerous time of all. Jay was not worried. Still he knew he would feel better when it was all over.

He glanced around the room again. No one had moved. They were all in the same places as when he had looked before.

A word the TV announcer said broke through Jay's thoughts. The word was "re-entry." Jay saw his mother stiffen for just an instant. Her eyes never left the screen. Her hand glided slowly up to her mouth and, without realizing it, she began to nibble on the tip of her finger.

Re-entry. Jay knew that could be one of the most risky parts of the flight. But Jay was sure his dad could handle it. He remembered that retrorockets slowed down the capsule so that it could leave its orbit and return to earth.

Suddenly Jay had to get up. He sprang to his feet and ran straight into Scotty's footstool.

"I'm a retrorocket!" he shouted.

That was all Scotty needed. He was restless anyway.

Soon both boys were racing around the room bumping into things and yelling, "I'm a retrorocket! I'm a retrorocket!"

The girls started to giggle and run after them.

But their mother was having none of that. She herded them back to their places in front of the TV set.

All four children were still giggling when the announcer reported that radio contact with the space capsule had been lost.

Jay and Scotty became suddenly silent. The girls kept laughing for a few seconds until they realized that their brothers had stopped. Then they were quiet too.

Jay knew that this was supposed to happen during the re-entry. The people at Cape Canaveral should be in touch with his dad again in about four or five minutes. He wasn't scared. He waited.

Then another report came through. The officials at Cape Canaveral were afraid the capsule might be coming in at a bad angle. It might not land where it was supposed to.

Jay sat down in one of the chairs in front of the set. Now he *was* scared a little. What if the angle really was bad? What if it got too hot inside the space capsule? What if . . . ?

Jay stopped himself in the middle of this last thought. He was perspiring as if he were up there in the capsule with his father. But there was nothing to worry about. His dad had said so.

Then Jay looked at the clock. More than five minutes had passed. The people at Cape Canaveral were not in touch

with his father yet. Why? Was something *really* wrong?

He glanced at his mother. She was sitting on the floor staring at the screen. Her mouth was opened slightly. Her fingers kept moving back and forth across her throat. He could see that she was worried.

Then the announcer said that the space capsule was not being picked up on radar.

Jay slumped down in his chair and his chin sank down on his chest. Scotty tried to make a joke, but nobody laughed. Even little Candy felt everyone's fears, and she climbed on her mother's lap.

Jay had to admit that he was scared now. He thought of things he and his dad wanted to do together, places they wanted to go. Then he remembered something that had happened just a few days before. Scotty had brought home a sick bird that he had found in the woods. The boys were going to nurse it back to health and let it go when it was able to fly again. But the bird had died.

Jay glanced at his mother. Her expression hadn't changed. She was still sitting in exactly the same spot. She said matter-of-factly, "I know he's down now, but the capsule is out of tracking range."

Jay was worried, but at the same time, he was thinking about how he and Dad would discuss the whole thing later. Dad would explain what had happened.

The announcer said that rescue teams were searching the spot in the Atlantic Ocean where the capsule should have come down.

Please find him, Jay thought. He could picture the destroyers, planes, and helicopters searching the ocean for a tiny speck that might be his father. He could picture his father all alone on a life raft, scanning the empty skies for some sign of help.

How will they ever find him? Jay found himself wondering, even as he was remembering his father telling him about all the ways that would be used to locate him.

Suddenly, Jay became aware of loud noises going on all around him. Scotty was shouting something at him, but Jay couldn't quite make out the words. Then his mind cleared.

". . . spotted!" Scotty was yelling. "They've spotted him in the Atlantic Ocean. He's safe!"

Jay leaped from his chair and joined in the laughing and shouting. He could hardly wait to see his dad to ask him more about those fireflies, or snowflakes, or whatever they were.

1

ACTIVITY **Fact Questions**

In reading a story, it is important that you notice clearly stated facts. Find out how well you grasped this kind of information. The answers are in the story, but try first to give your answer without looking back. Write on a separate piece of paper.

1. How many children were in the Carpenter family?

2. Which one was the eldest?

3. Where was the launching pad of the rocket?

4. Where were the Carpenters when Scott Carpenter took off in the rocket?

5. How did Jay spend most of the morning?

6. Who had a copy of the flight plan?

7. Name one of the experiments or observations that were in the flight plan.

8. What does a retrorocket do to a capsule?

9. Did the capsule land where it was supposed to land?

10. Where were rescue teams searching?

ACTIVITY 2
Thought Questions

Not all meanings in a story are stated directly in words. Sometimes you need to think about what you read.

As you think about the questions below, you will find meanings that are not directly stated in the story. Write your answers on a separate piece of paper.

1. Why do you think that the hours passed so slowly for the Carpenter family on the afternoon of the flight?

2. Why do you think Candy and Krissie seemed bored?

3. What do you think a flight plan probably is?

4. How could Jay hear his father's voice from the capsule?

5. Why was re-entry so important?

6. If the retrorockets did not work at all, what do you suppose would happen?

7. If the capsule left its orbit and headed for earth at the wrong angle, what might happen?

8. How did Jay know his mother was worried?

9. How did Mrs. Carpenter try to reassure the children?

10. What made Jay think of the dead bird?

ACTIVITY 3
Understanding Plot in a Story

The following events are not in order. On a separate sheet of paper, write the numbers of the events in the order in which they really happened. The event that happened first is #2.

1. Scott Carpenter phoned from the capsule.

2. Scotty brought home a sick bird.

3. Scott Carpenter saw particles of light that looked like snowflakes.

4. The rocket ship rose into the air.

5. Rescue teams searched for Scott Carpenter.

6. Jay learned that his father had been spotted.

7. Cape Canaveral lost radio contact with the space capsule.

**HOW TO READ IN
SOCIAL STUDIES**

The next selection is much like the information you might find in a social studies book. The way you read it is different from the way you read literature or science or mathematics. The illustrations in social studies readings are often just as important as the text. You may have to leave the reading, look at an illustration and study it, and then return to the same place in the text. Be sure you study all the pictures, graphs, and charts when you are reading in social studies.

You may have to do one of these in your social studies reading:

1. Look for *causes* of events and *results*.
2. Keep events in a *time sequence*.
3. *Compare* things that are alike or *contrast* things that are different.

In this selection, we are going to pay close attention to keeping events in a time sequence. You will find a cause-effect reading and a compare-contrast reading in other units of this book.

Keeping events in a *time sequence* means remembering the order in which they happened. In this way, we understand more clearly how one event leads to another. Dates are important clues to the time sequence.

Whenever you see letters change in size, shape, or thickness, you know that the word is important. Subheads can be helpful in social studies readings and other schoolwork.

In "Amelia Earhart," the next reading, you can find out some of the sequence of events by looking just at the subheads. To prove this, do the following:

1. Read the subheads in order. Do not stop to read anything else. Read only the subheads and notice how each one tells us something about Amelia Earhart's life.
2. Do Activity 1 at the end of the reading. You should be able to arrange the events in the right order even without reading the whole selection.

Now go on to read the whole article. Read each subhead again, then the part of the selection that follows it. Make sure that you read all the illustrations. After you have finished reading, go on to Activity 2.

Scott Carpenter was a hero, and members of his family had to be heroic, too. What makes a hero or a heroine? It takes an extraordinary amount of bravery as well as unusual achievement. Read to find out if Amelia Earhart was that kind of person.

Amelia Earhart

Written for this book
by Joseph H. Dempsey.

Progress depends on brave people who dare to do what no one has done before. One such person was Amelia Earhart, the first woman to fly alone across the Atlantic Ocean.

A Different Kind of Girl

Amelia Earhart was born on July 24, 1898, in Atchison, Kansas. Her parents may have known very soon that Amelia was going to be different. When many other girls were having make-believe tea parties, Amelia was jumping off her father's barn, using an umbrella as a parachute. When some girls were playing with dolls, Amelia was building a roller coaster on the roof of her father's tool shed.

Natal (nə tal'), seaport on the northeast coast of Brazil

Surinam (soor'i näm'), formerly Dutch Guiana; located on the northeast coast of South America

Dakar (dä kär'), capital and seaport of Senegal in northwest Africa

New Guinea (nōō gin'ē), a large island in the East Indies, north of Australia

Amelia began to get interested in airplanes at the age of 19. At that time, she was working as a nurses' aide in a Canadian military hospital. One of Amelia's friends was a pilot in the Royal Flying Corps. During her free time, Amelia used to go to a nearby airfield to watch him fly. She begged him to take her up in the airplane, but that was against regulations.

Falling in Love with Flying

Amelia's first plane ride took place later, in 1920, near Los Angeles, California. She fell in love with flying and began flying lessons immediately. This was a dangerous pastime. The engines of early airplanes were not much bigger than a modern motorcycle engine. In the first two months of flying, Amelia had two crash landings. Amelia was not reckless though. She simply loved to fly and was willing to face the hazards. Her instructors said that she was a natural pilot.

Amelia wanted to spend all her time

at the airfield, but she had to earn a living. She worked for the Los Angeles telephone company and saved money to buy her own airplane. She was finally able to buy a small plane in 1922.

Breaking the First Flying Record

One day, she invited her father and her sister to an air show. The two were sitting in the grandstands, watching the daring flyers above them, when they heard an announcement on the loudspeaker. The announcer said that young Amelia Earhart was going to try to break the women's altitude record. As her father and sister watched worriedly, Amelia's little plane went up and up and up — to 14,000 feet. She had broken the record! That was to be only the first of many new records.

Next, Amelia became a social worker. She was helping underprivileged children, but she still dreamed of flying. In 1927, Charles A. Lindbergh made his famous flight across the Atlantic Ocean. So Amelia could not be the first to do that. But she could be the first woman passenger to fly the Atlantic — and she was.

Nevertheless, being a passenger was nothing like being the pilot. In May of 1932, Amelia flew alone, non-stop, from Newfoundland, Canada, to Ireland. So she became the first woman to fly solo across the Atlantic Ocean.

Fame

Now the records began to fall fast. In August 1932, Amelia flew from Los Angeles, California, to Newark, New Jersey, in 19 hours and 5 minutes. This broke the women's non-stop transcontinental speed record. She broke the record again the following year by flying the same route in 17 hours and 7 minutes.

In January of 1935, Amelia became the first person to fly alone from Honolulu, Hawaii, across the Pacific Ocean to the U.S. mainland. Three months later, she became the first person to fly non-stop from Los Angeles to Mexico City. Then she became the first to fly non-stop from Mexico City to Newark, New Jersey.

By now, Amelia was famous. Purdue University in Lafayette, Indiana, asked her to join the faculty to act as adviser to the women studying at the university. Amelia jumped at the opportunity. She knew that women were as capable as men and believed that they "must earn true respect and equal rights from men by accepting responsibility."

The Greatest Challenge

Meanwhile, Amelia was planning for the greatest challenge yet — a 27,000-mile flight around the world. Wiley Post had already made the trip on a route north of the equator. On another flight, both he and Will Rogers, his famous passenger, were killed. Amelia planned to take a different route.

For this flight, Amelia would need perfect navigation. She planned to cross thousands of miles of open sea. The smallest error could mean death. She was not as good a navigator as she was a pilot. So she asked Fred Noonan to go with her. He was a pilot and navigator for Pan American Airways.

On May 17, 1937, the two took off from Oakland, California. They expected to fly around the world and re-

turn to Oakland in about six weeks. They arrived in Miami, Florida, on May 23, after making two stops along the way. There the plane was carefully checked.

From Miami they flew to Natal, Brazil, stopping at Puerto Rico, Venezuela, and Surinam. They knew that from Natal to Dakar in Senegal was the shortest flight to Africa. After missing it the first time, they landed at Dakar. Then they crossed the entire continent of Africa, hopping from city to city. India was ahead!

They flew to Calcutta and on to Rangoon and Singapore. After many more stops, they finally reached the island of New Guinea. Now the most dangerous part of the flight lay before them.

Amelia and Fred would have to fly 2,556 miles across the Pacific to land on tiny Howland Island. Finding the little island would not be easy. If they were not on target, they would be lost at sea.

The plane was loaded with enough gasoline for 4,000 miles, unless, of course, they ran into storms. A coast guard cutter was stationed near Howland to watch for them.

An Unsolved Mystery

It was July 2 when they took off for Howland Island. What happened after that no one knows. Somewhere between New Guinea and Howland Island the plane disappeared. The search for Amelia Earhart and Fred Noonan went on and on, but no trace of them was ever found.

Now planes fly daily over the routes that were so dangerous in 1937. The airplanes are much different from the plane Amelia Earhart flew. The instruments for navigating are far better than those used by Fred Noonan. We have made great progress in aviation. Some of that progress has to be credited to people like Amelia Earhart.

ACTIVITY 1

Here are the headings you just read, out of order. On your own paper, list the numbers of the headings in the order in which they occur in the story. The first one is #2.

1. Falling in Love with Flying
2. A Different Kind of Girl
3. The Greatest Challenge
4. Fame
5. Breaking the First Flying Record
6. An Unsolved Mystery

ACTIVITY 2

Working with a Time Line

This is a time line showing the years from Amelia's birth to July 2, 1937, when she disappeared. The questions may be answered by looking at the time line.

1. In what year did Amelia buy her own plane?

2. In what century was Amelia born? (Remember that we live in the 20th century.)

3. In May, 1932, what was Amelia's accomplishment?

4. Which happened first, her solo flight from Hawaii to the mainland or her record-breaking transcontinental flight?

5. Amelia became interested in planes at the age of 19. If you placed that on the time line, it would have to go immediately after (choose one):
   a. 1898 **b.** 1920 **c.** 1922

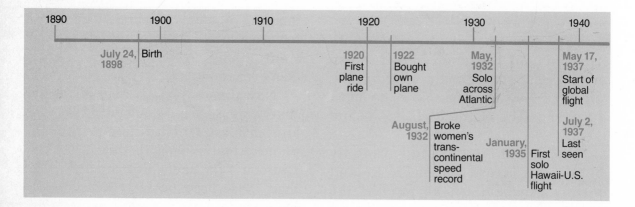

3 ACTIVITY

Getting Information from a Map

An important reading skill needed in social studies is the ability to read a map. The map you will be looking at is called a polar projection map. It gives you a better idea of Amelia Earhart's trip than you would get from a flat map. This kind of map is very important in our air-minded age. It gives you a truer picture of the earth's surface.

Write the answers to these questions on your paper.

1. Amelia Earhart landed at Calcutta. In what country is Calcutta?

2. Fred Noonan and Amelia missed Dakar on their first try. What is the name of a nearby group of islands where they could have landed?

3. Over what ocean was the flight from Natal to Dakar?

4. The last place she landed before reaching New Guinea was Darwin. On what continent is Darwin?

5. Amelia started her flight in North America. Name the other continents involved in the flight.

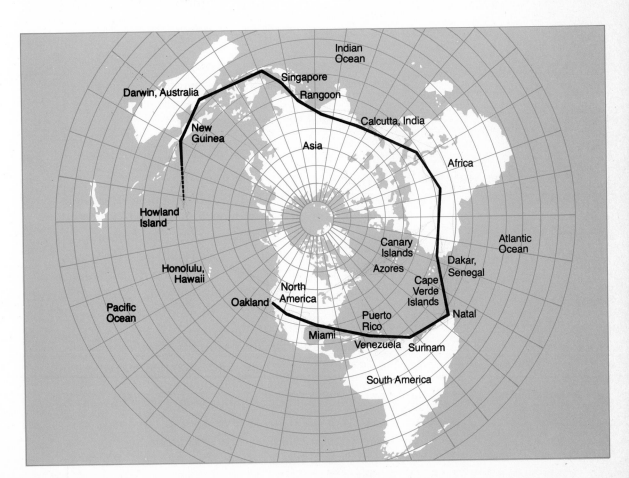

HOW TO READ IN SCIENCE

Making a Preview

In science books you often find diagrams that help in explaining some point that the author wishes to make. You also often find charts. Sometimes these charts show elements contained in different substances. Sometimes the charts show figures representing distances or quantities. You need to read these diagrams and charts differently from the way you read paragraphs.

In science you also often find headings over sections of the reading matter. These headings should be very useful to you. Sometimes they tell you the topic that is to be discussed in the next paragraph or paragraphs. Often they give you a summary of an important point or points made in the paragraphs.

One of the most useful things that you can do is to read the title, diagrams, charts, and headings before you read the article or chapter as a whole. This is called *previewing*.

Preview the article below before you read the paragraphs in the article. You will be surprised to see how much you can learn just by previewing.

1. Previewing the Title

In reading science material or any other reading material, read the title first of all. Think about it. It tells you the subject that will be discussed.

2. Previewing the Diagram

   a. Look at the diagram.

   b. Notice the title of the diagram.

   c. Study the diagram. What is in the center? Read the names of the planets around the center. How many are there? Notice the distance from the sun of each planet. Which is nearest? Which farthest? Do you suppose differences in the size of the dots have any meaning? Now cover the diagram with a piece of paper and do Activity 1.

3. Previewing the Headings

   a. Read the headings. Don't read the paragraphs below the headings at all. Just read each heading and think carefully about what it tells you.

   b. Cover the entire article with paper and do Activity 2.

4. After you have done your preview, read the article carefully to get additional facts and ideas that you didn't get during your preview.

5. Do Activity 3.

Amelia Earhart was one of the first to explore the sky. We made another leap into space when we sent a man to the moon. Now we are aiming for Mars. Later we may reach the other planets. Perhaps in your lifetime, a trip to one of the planets will be made as easily as we now circle our own globe. If you should ever have the chance to go to a planet, what do you think you will find there? This story will help you guess.

The Solar System _____

Written for this book
by Maurice U. Ames.

The solar system contains the sun and nine planets

The earth is a part of the solar system. *Solar* is from the Latin word meaning *sun*. The solar system is made up mainly of the sun and the nine planets that travel around the sun. The earth is only a tiny part of this system. Also, the whole solar system is only a very tiny part of the enormous universe. Our sun is just one of the many billions of stars in the universe.

The sun makes life on earth possible

The sun is very hot. It gives off both light and heat produced within itself. The energy which the earth gets from the sun makes it possible for us to live. All the fuels which run automobiles and heat houses contain energy from the sun. All of our food contains energy from the sun. If the sun were to burn out, the earth would soon become cold, dark, and without life of any kind.

The diagram shows the path of each of the nine planets as they travel around the sun. Such a path is called an *orbit*. Planets are held in their orbits by the balancing of two forces. One is the force of gravity, which prevents them from sailing out into space. The other is *centrifugal* force, which pulls away from the center, thus keeping the planets away from the sun.

Mercury is the smallest planet

On the diagram shown, if we look outward from the sun, we see first the planet Mercury. This is the smallest of all the planets. It is also the fastest in its movement around the sun. It travels around the sun once in 88 of our days. The length of time it takes a planet to circle the sun is known as its *year*. Mercury's year is, therefore, 88 of our days.

Venus is the brightest

The next planet we come to is Venus. It is often called the *sister* of the earth. Venus is about the same size as the earth. It is only slightly smaller. Venus was named for the ancient goddess of beauty because it is the brightest planet in our sky. It can be seen in the morning and early evening.

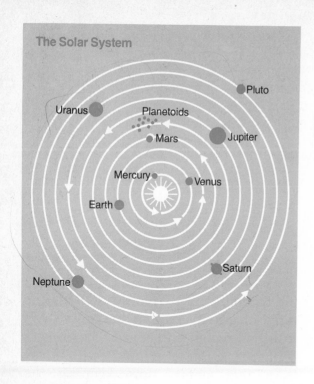

The Solar System

which can be observed with telescopes from the earth. Through telescopes they have discovered that Mars goes through seasons like the earth. At this time, however, there is no real proof of life on Mars. You will hear more about this in your lifetime.

Jupiter is the largest planet

The largest of all the "children" of the sun is the giant planet Jupiter. Its diameter is more than ten times that of the earth. Heavy clouds encircle Jupiter near its equator. Scientists think that the surface temperature of Jupiter is about 200° below zero. Jupiter has 12 moons.

The earth has a satellite

The next member of the planet family is our own earth. The earth is the fifth largest planet. It is the third planet from the sun. It takes a little more than 365 days for the earth to revolve around the sun. The earth has a little follower, the moon, which revolves around the earth.

A body that revolves around a larger body in the sky is called a *satellite*. The moon is a satellite of the earth. Many manufactured satellites, shot up by great rockets, are now circling the earth, hundreds of miles out in space.

Mars goes through seasons

Mars is smaller than the earth. It takes Mars almost twice as long as the earth to circle around the sun. Mars is reddish in color. Because of this fiery color the ancient Romans named it after the god of war. Mars is better known by scientists than any of the other planets

Saturn has three rings and nine moons

Saturn is an unusual planet. It has three rings which encircle it at its equator. The three rings are made up of small satellites whose orbits are very close together. They may be the result of the explosions of moons which encircled the planet at one time. Since these bodies are very close together the rings appear to be a solid mass. In addition to the three rings, Saturn also has nine moons.

Uranus, Neptune, and Pluto are farthest away

Uranus, Neptune, and Pluto are the planets farthest away from the sun and earth. They can be seen only with a telescope and were discovered only within the last two centuries.

Uranus was discovered in 1781 by an English astronomer. At first he thought it was a comet. Neptune was discovered in 1846 by two astronomers who believed that another planet was pulling on Uranus. With mathematics, they were able to tell just where this new planet was located.

Pluto was observed first in 1930. These outermost planets take a long time to circle once around the sun. One "year" on Pluto is equal to 248 of our years on earth. Scientists know less about Pluto than about the other planets. Its yellow color, however, suggests that this planet probably has very little atmosphere.

ACTIVITY 1

On a separate sheet of paper, answer these questions to see how much you got from previewing the diagram.

1. Tell in three words what the diagram shows.
2. Which planet is nearest to the sun?
3. Which is farthest away from the sun?
4. How many planets revolve around the sun?
5. Name these planets.

ACTIVITY 2

Find out how much information you got from reading the headings. The first few words of each heading are given below. On your own paper, copy each one and finish it.

1. The solar system contains. . . .
2. The sun makes life. . . .
3. Mercury is. . . .
4. Venus is. . . .
5. The earth has a. . . .
6. Mars goes. . . .
7. Jupiter is. . . .
8. Saturn has. . . .
9. Uranus, Neptune, and Pluto. . . .

ACTIVITY 3

Try to answer these questions without looking back at the article. If you have to look back, the headings will help you.

1. What is the solar system?
2. Why would the earth be without life if the sun were to burn out?
3. Which planet is better known by scientists than any of the other planets which can be observed by telescope from the earth?
4. What is a satellite?
5. What is the earth's satellite?
6. What are manufactured satellites?
7. Upon what is the length of year for any planet based?
8. What is an *orbit*?
9. What may have caused the three rings around Saturn?
10. What were the last planets to be discovered?

**HOW TO READ IN
MATHEMATICS**

Did you ever stop to think how much *reading* you have to do when you study mathematics? To do good work in mathematics you need to know how to do a different kind of reading. It is not the same as reading stories or reading in social studies or science.

Reading numerals is one special kind of reading that you have to do in mathematics. It is especially important in the space age that you know how to read numerals of four, five, or six digits. You will now be given special help in reading and understanding large numerals.

A long time ago, people probably began writing numbers by scratching a straight line in clay with a stick. Each scratch meant one man or one deer or one of something. That was easy to understand. Now that we plan to travel in space, we are using large numbers for things that are not easy to picture. Can you picture 238,857 miles? Yet that is the distance to the moon, and we put a man there.

Are you ready to handle space-age numbers? This reading will help.

Babylonian Numerals

Written for this book
by William L. Schaaf.

The ancient Babylonians were among the first people to develop numerals, that is, numbers expressed in writing. The Babylonians used two symbols for their numerals. They used this symbol for one ▼ . They used this symbol for ten ◄ . Here are some examples of Babylonian numerals.

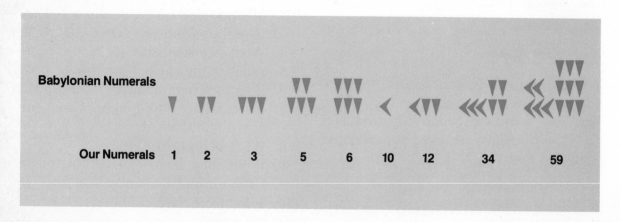

Babylonian Numerals									
Our Numerals	1	2	3	5	6	10	12	34	59

ACTIVITY 1

1. On your own paper, write each of the following in Babylonian numerals. First decide how many tens and ones are in each number. You may then write the Babylonian numeral in one straight line going across the page. For example, 39 stands for 3 tens and 9 ones. You would write this as: «‹ʸʸʸʸʸʸʸʸʸ

   a. 7
   b. 28
   c. 56

2. What problem would the Babylonians have had in writing the large numerals our space scientists must use, numerals in the millions, billions, and trillions?

Why Is Zero Important?

Did you notice that the Babylonians did not have a symbol for zero? Zero is the most important symbol in our numeral system. None of the ancient peoples had a symbol for zero. In fact, this important symbol has been used for only about 1,000 years.

Why is zero so important in our numeral system? Think about the zero in the numeral 105. Suppose we left out the zero and wrote this numeral as 15. Is there a difference between 105 and 15?

ACTIVITY 2

Write your answers on your own paper.

   a. 50 is how many more than 5?
   b. 10 is how many more than 1?
   c. 60 is how many times greater than 6?
   d. 700 is how many times greater than 70?

Zero does two things. In the numeral 605, zero shows that there are *no tens*. It also is a *place-holder* for the tens place. Without zero we would not have a place-holder. We would not have a place-value numeral system.

If a 5 is placed in the tens column, it is worth ten times as much as a 5 placed in the ones column. If a 5 is placed in the hundreds column, it is worth ten times as much as a 5 placed in the tens column.

In the sentences which follow, you will find numbers written out in words. Make columns on your own paper with headings as in the example below. Look at the number given in words in each sentence. Write each one on your paper, using numerals placed in the correct column. Be sure to use zero as a place-holder. The first one is done for you as an example.

1. Our moon is about *two hundred twenty thousand* miles from the earth when it is nearest to the earth.
2. In sixty hours, the moon moves more than *one hundred thirty-five thousand* miles.
3. Pluto is about *three billion, five hundred million* miles from the earth.
4. Mars is about *forty-eight million* miles from the earth.
5. The star nearest to earth is more than *twenty-five trillion* miles away.

	TRILLIONS	BILLIONS	MILLIONS	THOUSANDS	UNITS
	100's 10's 1's	100's 10's 1's	100's 10's 1's	100's 10's 1's	100's 10's 1's
1.	— — —,	— — —,	— — —,	2 2 0,	0 0 0

Finding the Main Idea in a Paragraph

Finding the main idea in a paragraph is a valuable reading skill. This skill will be helpful to you in all your studies. The main idea is a statement that includes most of the other ideas. For example, the idea "building" includes "house," "school," "garage," and many other kinds of buildings. In a paragraph, look for a sentence that includes the ideas of the other sentences.

In each paragraph below, one sentence includes the ideas of the rest of the paragraph. It sums up the paragraph. See if you can find this sentence.

Below each paragraph, you will find three ideas that are expressed in the paragraph. Decide which one you think is the main idea of the paragraph. Write the letter of that statement on your paper.

The Fascinating Sun

1. The surface of the sun looks like a sea of white-hot clouds. These clouds are not made of water vapor. They are made of copper, iron, calcium, sodium, and other substances. These substances, however, do not exist in solid forms on the sun. Because of the hot temperatures, they are gases. That's why the sun appears to be covered with bright clouds.
   a. The sun is hot.
   b. These clouds are not made of water vapor.
   c. The surface of the sun looks like a sea of clouds.

2. The surface of the sun appears rough and flaky. When astronomers look at it through a telescope, they see something that looks like snowflakes on gray cloth. These flakes are from 400 to 600 miles in diameter. They appear in many different shapes and change continuously. Old ones go out of sight. New ones come into view. But always they cause the surface to look rough.
   a. These flakes are from 400 to 600 miles in diameter.
   b. The surface of the sun appears rough and flaky.
   c. Old ones go out of sight.

3. Dark spots, called sunspots, can be seen on the sun at times. Sunspots are really whirlpools in the gases on the surface of the sun. These sunspots have a dark central portion and a lighter outer portion. Many of these sunspots last for only about 24 hours. Very few can be seen for longer than a week.
   a. They have a dark central portion.
   b. Dark spots can be seen on the sun at times.
   c. Many sunspots last for only about 24 hours.

More About Finding Main Ideas

In working with the next article, you will have more practice in finding main ideas. Do this:
1. Read each paragraph carefully.
2. After reading it, find the sentence that gives the one most important thought. Write that sentence on your paper after the letter of the paragraph.

Gifts of the Nile

A. The Nile is a watery highway, carrying traffic of all kinds for the people of Egypt. Flat-bottomed boats carry fruits and vegetables from one city to another. There are also passenger boats on the Nile. These boats carry people up and down the river. Very heavy loads can travel by barges. In ancient times, huge blocks of stone were floated down the river on barges. The stone was used to make buildings and monuments.

B. The Nile also provides food for the people of Egypt. Egypt is mostly a desert. Crops will not grow in this desert land. But close to the Nile, crops grow well. In fact, several different crops are often raised on the same land during one year. Water from the Nile helps make the land fertile.

C. The Nile's yearly floods used to benefit the people. Rain falls heavily in the Ethiopian mountains and highlands. The water from these rains flows down into the Nile. The river swells and rises. These early summer rains used to cause floods. The river overflowed its banks and spread over the land. It carried rich soil inland every summer. It also brought water for crops. Fields were more productive after the flood.

D. Now dams prevent floods. Water rises high in the river every summer, as always. The water does not overflow the riverbanks, however. A series of dams stores the water. The Aswan Dam is the largest one. It is more than a mile long and about 176 feet high. With the help of dams, Egyptians can use the water year round, not just at flood time.

E. Egyptians lead the waters of the Nile to their fields in several different ways. Canals and ditches lead out from the river to the farms. Some people lift water in buckets and jars if the level is low. In other places, electric pumps draw out the water.

F. Because of the Nile, Egyptians had the opportunity to create a civilization early in history. In its 4,000-mile-long valley, farmers grow crops for food and cotton for clothing. Mud from the river bottom makes good bricks for houses. Life was a little easier for people by the Nile. They did not have to work as hard as other people for their food, clothing, and shelter. They had more time for thinking, inventing, and creating. These activities— thinking, inventing, and creating— make a civilization.

Working with Compound Words

A compound word, as you know, is made up of two or more words. The meaning of a compound word is different from either of the words which it contains.

Bob wants to write for a newspaper. A newspaper writer must make his stories as short as he can. Help Bob shorten his story below. Words which you can use to make compound words are underlined. On your own paper, write the number that appears before each group of underlined words. After the number, write the compound word you made up from the underlined words. (The first answer is horseback.)

Dick Carter went riding (1) on the back of a horse across the (2) side of the mountain last Sunday (3) during the time of day after noon. He was listening to the singing of a (4) bird which is blue when he heard the sound of (5) steps made by the foot behind him. Then he heard a cry for help.

Dick turned and saw a man running toward him. "Thank goodness you're here," the man cried. "I'm Harry Brown, an airplane pilot. My plane crashed on the (6) side of the hill a week ago."

Dick gave Mr. Brown his canteen of water, which he had brought as a (7) guard to keep someone safe against thirst. "I'll bring help," he said.

Dick raced back toward town, across (8) land with grass growing on it and around (9) ponds with fish in them. He paid no attention to branches (10) hanging over the path above him or mud (11) under his horse's foot. He didn't slow down till he reached the (12) step in front of the door of the (13) house in which a law court is held. "Come quickly!" he shouted.

After he was rescued, Mr. Brown said, "I've been living on (14) berries which are black and (15) nuts from the hazel tree all week. I can't wait to have a big, juicy (16) steak of beef!"

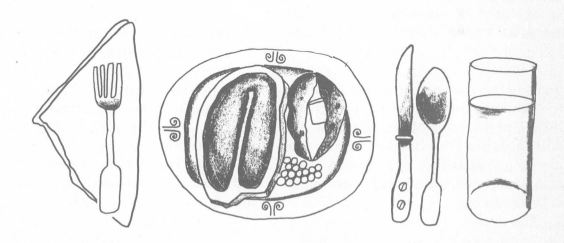

Critical Reading

If you are to become a highly skilled reader, you must learn to do critical reading. In doing critical reading you form your own opinion of what you read. You think carefully about what is said and then place your own value on parts of it. You decide for yourself what in the article or chapter is accurate, true, fair, or just. Often you will need to do more reading to get additional facts for making such decisions.

◼ Beware of the Snare in Ads

One important area in which we should be especially critical is advertising. Law prevents out-and-out lies in advertising. Yet there are many ways we can be deceived. One of these is the clever use of words.

It's not true that "sticks and stones will break my bones, but words will never hurt me." Words *can* hurt because they make us believe things that are not true. In this reading, we will look at some of the slippery words advertisers use to deceive us. When you see any of these, be especially alert.

LIKE

It's like having your own private lake.

Close your eyes for a minute and think of the line you just read above. What did you think of? Did you picture a quiet lake, water gently rippling, shining only for you? You're not unusual. That is what many people would think. The thought of "private lake" is so powerful it simply expands in our heads and pushes out that little word "like."

Yet "like" is the most important word in the sentence. It means "similar to." You are not being offered a private lake. You are being offered a similarity, a likeness to a lake. In other words, you are being offered an appearance, a resemblance, something that is not what it seems to be.

The ad did not make any false promises. Our own minds provided the deception. We seem to have a tendency to be hooked by striking, vivid words and to overlook their dull companions.

Here's another example of the power of striking words:

It's like having a tiger in your tank.

It's amusing to think of a tiger in the tank of a car. It would be truly wonderful to control the strength and ferocity of a tiger. It is so much fun to think about this that we forget that the subject is not tigers at all — it's gasoline.

And while hooked on this daydream, we forget to ask questions that might really help us. Why is this gasoline better than others? Does a car get more miles to the gallon? Is this gas cheaper? Is it better for the engine? In fact, is there any good reason to buy this gasoline?

The ad offers us no reasons. But we didn't notice. We were too busy thinking about tigers.

HELP

"Help" is another word much used in advertising. Did you ever notice it in

Helps fight cavities . . .
Helps build strong bodies . . .
Helps prevent dandruff . . .

You never noticed it before? Then why is it there? Because with it, ads appear to make claims. For instance, suppose the ad said, "This shampoo prevents dandruff." Then people who used the shampoo and still had dandruff might feel they had been cheated. They might start lawsuits against the people who said their dandruff would go away. And they might win.

A truthful ad might read like this: "This shampoo prevents dandruff for some people who have no skin diseases and no stress in their daily lives, who wash neither too much nor too little, who do not get too much sun and do not wear hats constantly and do not use another person's comb or brush."

But who would listen to such a long ad? No one. So the advertiser plugs in the word "helps." It is safe to say that a shampoo "helps" if there is one person somewhere it has helped. Many advertisers can say that much.

Whenever you see the word "helps," remember that the sentence should probably be followed by a long list of other things that also help. For instance, perhaps bread helps build strong bodies *if* you also eat many other kinds of good foods, exercise, breathe fresh air, and get enough sleep. Perhaps a toothpaste helps fight cavities *if* you don't eat too many sweets, don't chew gum, brush regularly and often, visit your dentist, and follow all the other rules for good teeth.

CAN

Another little word we often overlook is "can."

OUT can remove spots in seconds!

Notice that the ad does not claim that OUT *will* remove spots—only that it *can*. Nor does it say that OUT will always do it in seconds—only that it *can*. Perhaps OUT will remove spots only in cotton clothes. Perhaps OUT will remove only ink spots. Perhaps OUT can remove one kind of spot in seconds, others in hours. Perhaps OUT removes spots only in hot water. The ad does not tell us the whole truth.

◤ ACTIVITY 1

Here are some imaginary ads. In each, find a word you should not overlook. It will be "can" or "like" or "help" or "helps." Write it after the number on your own paper.

1. Give your child Encyclopedia Ripoff! With it, your child can win a scholarship to college!

2. Switch to Koffs! A cigarette that helps fight dullness.

3. Buy Starp! Like making your floors hospital-clean!

4. Slosh can be of enormous benefit in a program of dental hygiene.

5. A Yamahokomoko motorcycle helps make a little guy into a big fellow.

Reviewing the Sounds of Consonants _____

A. Can you tell a consonant when you see it at one quick glance? Being able to recognize consonants quickly will help you in pronouncing new words.

Here is the alphabet. The letters *a, e, i, o,* and *u* are vowels. All the other letters are consonants.

a b c d e f g h i j k l m n o p q r s t u v w x y z

1. On your own paper, write the consonants. Sometimes *y* is used as a vowel. Think of *y* as a consonant here.

2. How many consonants are there?

B. The name of each picture below begins with a different consonant sound.

Look at each picture. Say its name to yourself. With what sound does the name start? Find the letter beneath the picture that stands for that sound. Write that letter on your paper after the number in the same box.

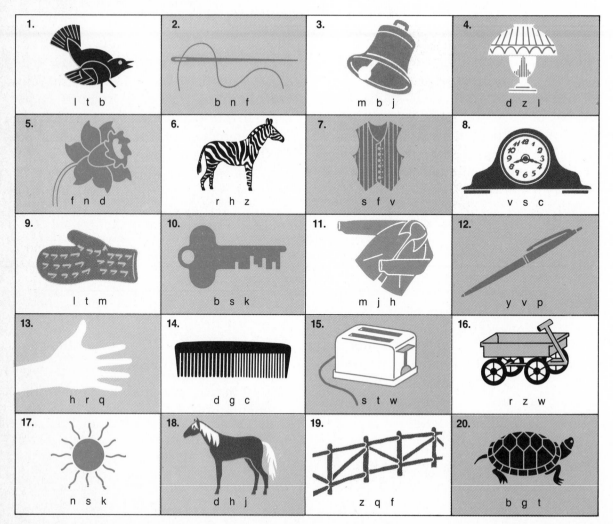

1. l t b	**2.** b n f	**3.** m b j	**4.** d z l
5. f n d	**6.** r h z	**7.** s f v	**8.** v s c
9. l t m	**10.** b s k	**11.** m j h	**12.** y v p
13. h r q	**14.** d g c	**15.** s t w	**16.** r z w
17. n s k	**18.** d h j	**19.** z q f	**20.** b g t

Making Use of the Consonants

Follow the directions below to make a rhyme.

1. Find the words in Columns A, B, and C which *begin* with consonants. Write the words in order on your paper, reading down the columns. If the words are followed by commas, periods, or other punctuation marks, write those too. After every series of dots, begin a new line.

2. Find the words in Columns D, E, and F which *end* with consonants. Write them in order on your paper to finish the rhyme.

A	B	C	D	E	F
Are	rockets	the	If	you'll	world
Would	every	over	the	hoe	that
you	to	moon,	you	find	area
able	in	to	such	blue	will
like	Mars?	argues	cue	see	banana
and	To	discover	things	Views	blow
to	see	new	ever	of	your
fly	all	under	able	your	plea
ask	each	stars?	happen,	also	mind!

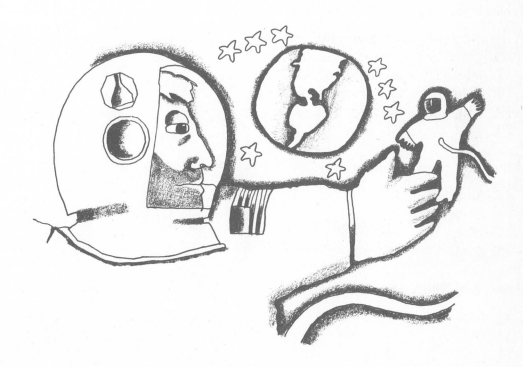

29

Long and Short Sounds of the Vowels

The vowels *a, e, i, o,* and *u* have two very common sounds. One of these is often called the "long" sound. This sound gives the name of the vowel as *a* in *age, e* in *be, i* in *like, o* in *go, u* in *music.* In dictionaries this sound is marked with a bar above it like this: āge.

Another common sound of each of these vowels is often called the "short" sound. Examples of this sound are: *a* as in *at, e* as in *set, i* as in *it, o* as in *on, u* as in *hut.* Most recent dictionaries do not mark the short sounds.

Some of the words below have long vowel sounds, and some have short vowel sounds.

Write the number of each word on your own paper. Write *l* after the number if the word has a long vowel. Write *s* if the vowel in the word is short.

Long and Short Sounds of *a*

1. flat
2. gas
3. trade
4. date
5. banks
6. planes
7. map
8. path

Long and Short Sounds of *e*

9. left
10. these
11. shed
12. we
13. best
14. veto
15. me
16. deck

Long and Short Sounds of *i*

17. wings
18. light
19. trip
20. mist
21. kite
22. ship
23. twice
24. line

Long and Short Sounds of *o*

25. most
26. globe
27. crop
28. post
29. stop
30. hot
31. own
32. trot

Long and Short Sounds of *u*

33. use
34. tub
35. cute
36. shut
37. crust
38. mule
39. rude
40. such

Recognizing Long and Short Vowel Sounds _____

The pilot of the new rocket ship returned to earth sooner than he was supposed to. Why? To find his explanation, use your knowledge of long and short vowel sounds. The answer is hidden below.

If the vowel sound of the word is short, write on your paper the letter next to the word. If the vowel sound is long, do nothing. Go on to the next word. The letters you write will tell what the pilot said.

1. space —O	**15.** best —G	**29.** shine —R	**43.** hot —W
2. flat —I	**16.** these —R	**30.** mist —E	**44.** phone —I
3. gas —W	**17.** deck —O	**31.** ship —M	**45.** tub —A
4. place —H	**18.** scene —S	**32.** wing —O	**46.** use —I
5. hat —A	**19.** flee —I	**33.** think —O	**47.** cute —L
6. gave —R	**20.** he —R	**34.** size —R	**48.** mule —D
7. match —N	**21.** well —T	**35.** hint —N	**49.** shut —S
8. path —T	**22.** blend —O	**36.** bus —B	**50.** crust —F
9. plane —S	**23.** give —T	**37.** crop —U	**51.** rule —R
10. map —E	**24.** light —A	**38.** post —L	**52.** such —U
11. banks —D	**25.** kite —S	**39.** lots —T	**53.** tube —C
12. left —T	**26.** trip —H	**40.** notch —I	**54.** must —L
13. be —H	**27.** twice —O	**41.** globe —H	**55.** mud —L
14. shed —O	**28.** line —A	**42.** stop —T	

Finding Long and Short Vowels in a Story _____

Some words have been left out of this story. Some of these are long-vowel words. Some are short-vowel words. These words are listed at the end of the story. Choose the correct word for each blank space, using the hint in parentheses. No word may be used twice. On your paper, write the word next to the number of the blank. For example, #1 is *huge*.

◼ The Monster Protected by King Minos

King Minos kept a monster in a winding passageway. This monster was a (1. long u sound) _____ creature that (2. long a sound) _____ helpless animals and (3. long u sound) _____ beings that Minos (4. long a sound) _____ in the passageway.

One day a fair-haired young (5. short a sound) _____ was sent to Minos as food for the monster. The king's daughter was sitting nearby. She (6. long a sound) _____ to have the young man (7. short e sound) _____ to the monster. She thought, "This monster (8. short u sound) _____ die!"

The king's daughter (9. long i sound) _____ the guards to (10. short e sound) _____ the young man (11. long o sound) _____ into the passageways that (12. long i sound) _____ . She (13. long a sound) _____ him a sharp sword. (14. long e sound) _____ also placed a small thin (15. long o sound) _____ in his hand. This rope would lead him back through the passageways.

The young man did as he was told. He found the monster and killed it. After this the people in the kingdom were happy the monster had been killed.

placed	ate	human	fed
rope	bribed	must	go
huge	man	gave	hated
let	she	night	

32

Working with Social Studies Words

The words below are among those which often appear in social studies books at your level. You will meet them frequently in your reading, both in and out of school.

Study the pronunciation of each of these words to make sure that you know how to pronounce it correctly. Say each word to yourself, pronouncing it distinctly. Then read the meaning of the word and think about it.

---

abolish (ə bol'ish), to do away with, put an end to completely

ancient (ān'shənt), having to do with times long ago

barbarian (bär bãr'ē ən), a person who is not civilized

caravan (kar'ə van), a group of people traveling together

craft (kraft), a trade or art requiring special skill

famine (fam'ən), lack of food, not enough food for all

monarch (mon'ərk), a king, queen, or emperor who rules a country alone

peasant (pez'nt), a farmer of the working class in Europe

prehistoric (prē'his tôr'ik), before history was written; before 3000 B.C.

rural (roor'əl), having to do with the country

Choose one of the words defined above to complete the meaning of each of the following sentences. On your paper, write each sentence with the blank filled in. You may have to add s to some of the words.

1. Greece was one of the _____ countries that had city-states.

2. Long _____ of people on camels can still be seen on the African desert.

3. Men could not read or write in _____ times.

4. Philip II ruled his lands by himself. He was a _____ .

5. There is not much farming land in Greece, but many people in that country are still _____ .

6. When a new king came into power, he would often _____ laws made by the king before him.

7. People who lived in the prehistoric period are sometimes called _____ .

8. Some of the early people worked at the _____ of making pottery.

9. Many people prefer _____ life to city life.

10. One year there was a flood that destroyed all of the food crops in a certain country. That year there was a _____ in this country.

Working with Mathematics Words

The words below appear in most mathematics books. You will be able to understand your lessons in mathematics better if you know the meanings and pronunciations of these words as they are used in mathematics. Check the pronunciations and meanings of the words below to make sure you know them.

Study the pronunciation of each word. Say the word to yourself. Then read and think about its meaning.

---

bisect (bī sekt'), to divide into two parts; in mathematics, to divide into two equal parts

cone (kōn), a solid that has a flat, round base and curved sides which narrow to a point at the top

cube (kūb), a solid with six square, equal sides

cylinder (sil'in dér), a solid or hollow usually in the shape of a tin can; has two flat circular bases, and the surface between them is curved

dimension (də men'shən), measurement of length, width, or thickness

hemisphere (hem'ə sfêr), half of a sphere or globe

pyramid (pir'ə mid), a solid, usually with a square or rectangular base, and four triangular sides meeting in a point at the top

sphere (sfêr), a solid shaped like a ball; every point on its surface is an equal distance from the center

---

Choose one of the words defined above to complete the meaning of some of the following sentences. On your paper, write each sentence with the blank filled in. You will need to add s to one of the words.

In some cases you will be asked to draw a figure.

1. The _____ of the table were: 5 feet long by 3½ feet wide.

2. If line *AB* cuts line *CD* in half, line *AB* is said to _____ line *CD*.

3. The globe that you use in geography is in the shape of a _____.

4. The half of the earth in which we live is called the Western _____.

5. Draw a pyramid.

6. Draw a cylinder.

7. Draw a cone.

8. Draw a cube.

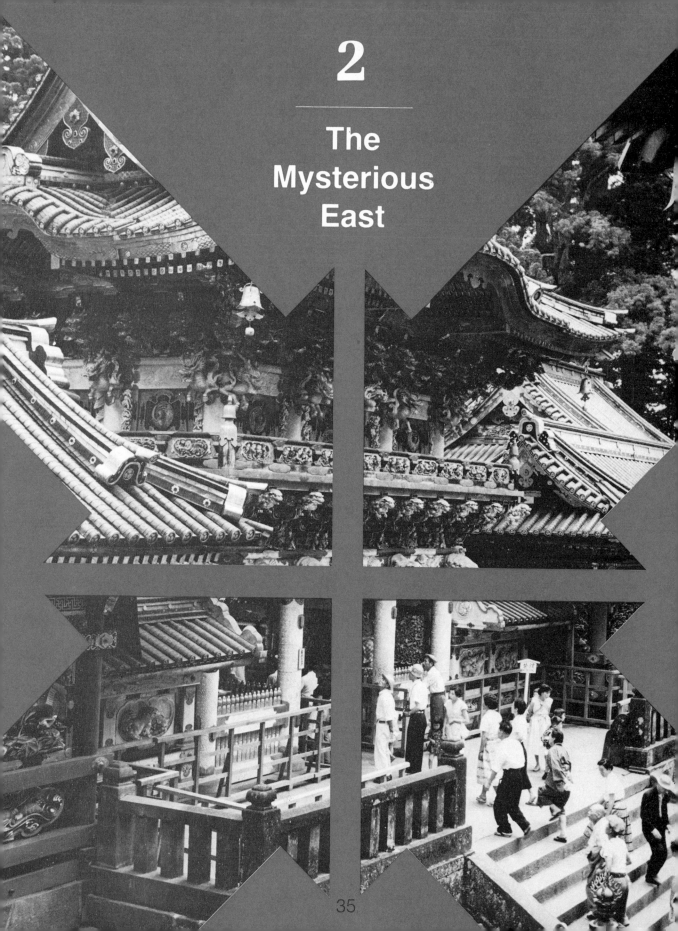

2

The
Mysterious
East

HOW TO READ LITERATURE

One of the important elements in a story is its setting. The time and place of a story are the setting. Sometimes the setting tells us a great deal about the people in a story.

For example, you may read in a story that a 45-year-old man always did what his father told him to do. In a story set in our time, such a man would be quite unusual. However, a few centuries ago, this kind of obedience was quite common. No matter what age people were, they felt they should obey their parents. As soon as you know the *time* of the story, your opinion of such a man changes. The *setting* changes the meaning for the reader.

In the same way, the place of a story can change the meaning of certain actions. A person who slurps noisily while drinking soup would be thought rude in the United States. In Japan, however, making noise while eating soup is good manners. It shows appreciation for a delicious dish. So the *place* of an action can change the meaning, too.

The setting is important in the story, "The Kimono." Look for all the signs of a different time or place in the story. The setting explains much of the problem Nori faces in "The Kimono."

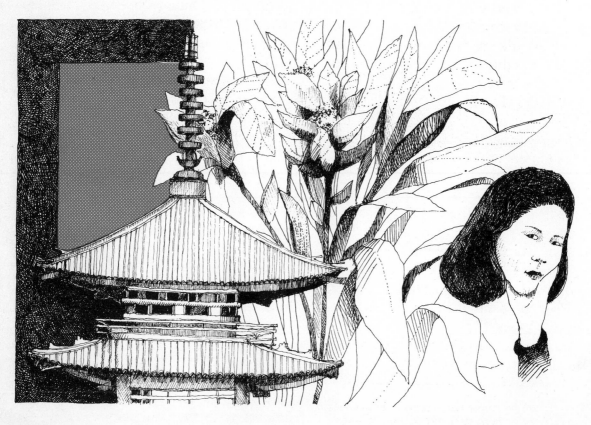

Did you ever have to move to a new town? Enter a new school? Find new friends in a place where you knew no one? That can be hard. It is harder still to do this in a foreign country. There everything is new and strange. A newcomer may be quite unhappy until—until what? What can make you feel at home in a foreign place? This story tells how one person found a way.

The Kimono

Written for this book
by Juliana O. Muehrcke.

"I give up!" Nori cried. She threw the spray of yellow flowers to the floor.

Her cousin Keiko opened her black eyes in amazement. Keiko had grown up in Japan and was not used to Nori's sudden American ways. Nori had never learned to hide her feelings, as Japanese girls are taught to do. Keiko did not know what to say.

"I'm sorry I shouted," Nori said. She bent to pick up the flowers. "It's just that I'll never learn to arrange flowers."

"Yes, you will," Keiko said gently. "It is the Japanese way."

"But that's just it!" Nori burst out again. "I'm not Japanese. I'm American. I was born in California, and I lived there all my life till now. My parents are Japanese and I look Japanese, but that makes it all the harder. Everyone expects me to do things the Japanese way. But I can't!"

All the anger Nori had felt these last few months came rushing out. She hadn't wanted to come to Japan in the first place. But when her grandmother had invited her to spend a year in Japan, Nori's father said it was a fine opportunity. Once Father had made up his mind, it was no use to argue. The word of the Japanese father is not questioned.

Once she was in Japan, Nori had honestly tried to be the sort of girl her grandmother wanted her to be. She had worked hard in school and at her lessons in flower-arranging. But her hands were clumsy and untrained. She seemed to do everything wrong.

"I think you are lucky to be both Japanese and American," Keiko said. "You have two homes and two languages. That is something special."

"You're the one that's lucky," said Nori. "You belong here. I don't."

Nori stuck a spray of yellow flowers in the white bowl as she had seen her teacher do many times. She had cut the branches in the Japanese way so that they were three different lengths. The flowers with the short stems stood for

---

kimono (kə mō′nə), loose outer garment with a sash, once worn by both men and women in Japan

the earth. The tall flowers, standing high above the others, stood for heaven. The medium-length flowers stood for human beings who link heaven and earth.

When heaven, man, and earth were in harmony, the flower arrangement succeeded. But Nori's didn't look the way it should. It was all wrong—again. And it seemed such a simple thing to do! *Why* couldn't she learn it? Wouldn't Nori ever be able to please her grandmother?

Nori sighed. "I hoped I could make a pretty flower arrangement for the party tonight," she said sadly. "It would have made Grandmother so happy."

Keiko's dark eyes danced at the thought of the party. "Are you going to wear the kimono your grandmother gave you?" she asked. "It is so beautiful."

"I know it is," Nori said. "But I wouldn't feel right wearing it." The long, flowing kimonos which many Japanese women wore to parties looked lovely on them. Kimonos were really much prettier than Western clothes, Nori thought. But she would make a fool of herself in a kimono. In a narrow kimono, you had to take short steps and keep your knees close together. Otherwise, the kimono would flap open. Nori was sure she would forget about walking properly. She would look clumsy and silly. Better not even try.

"It's time to go home and help my family get ready for the party," Keiko said. She jumped to her feet and crossed the room with quick, light steps.

Nori felt a stab of envy as she watched her cousin. Keiko would wear a kimono to the party tonight, and she would look beautiful and graceful. Keiko would know the right things to do and say, too. Manners were much more casual in America, Nori thought. Here it was important to do everything just so. And Nori seemed always to do the wrong thing.

After Keiko had gone, Nori felt tears in her eyes. She thought about her family back in California. More than anything, she wanted to feel like part of a family again. But she would never be accepted here—not when she couldn't even arrange a few flowers!

Nori picked up the flowers again. The words of her teacher came back to her: "You cannot arrange flowers well unless your heart is serene." That must be my problem, Nori thought. My heart is anything but serene.

Just then, Grandmother came into the room. Her arms were full of packages of food for the party.

"I smell rice burning!" Grandmother said.

Oh, dear! Nori suddenly remembered that she had put the rice on the stove to cook. She had hoped to please Grandmother by making the evening rice, but now the water had boiled away. The rice was black and burned.

Could she do nothing right?

Nori fled from the house. Once she was outside in the garden, she let the tears stream down her cheeks. She sank onto the soft moss and put her face in her hands. She had never felt so lost and alone.

It was very quiet. Her sobbing slowed. With a few sniffs, it stopped, and she wiped her eyes. She looked around the garden. How beautiful it was! A pine branch was reflected in the little pond. The cherry tree was a white fluff of blossoms.

It was a small yard, yet every inch of it was as pretty as a picture. Her grandmother had planned it that way. It was very Japanese, Nori knew, to draw from each thing its special beauty. The Japanese found joy in the smallest things. Things as simple and natural as the rising moon or a singing bird were treated as treasures. And so they really are, Nori suddenly thought.

Nori had been in the garden before, of course, but she had always been too busy to notice how carefully it was planned. Most other Americans would not notice it either, she thought. Americans worked too hard, moved too fast. People there never seemed to take time to look at the moon or a flower.

Perhaps she had been trying to move too fast, Nori thought. She had been in such a great hurry to learn everything and learn it right away. Maybe it was better to relax and find the beauty right here and now—in this passing moment. The Japanese knew there was comfort in beauty. Everyone could plan his life so there was beauty in it—just as there was beauty in this small garden. I'm lucky to be Japanese, Nori thought. Lucky to be here. Lucky just to be alive!

Nori hugged the warm feeling to her as she ran back inside. Her heart was so full of joy that she almost forgot to slip off her shoes at the door.

"Where is the pot I burned, Grandmother?" she asked. "I want to scrub it clean."

"I've done it for you," said Grandmother.

Nori waited for her to say more about the burned rice. Nori had been

acting like an American again—wasting food! But her grandmother just went on with preparations for dinner. She knows I can't help being what I am, Nori thought. I am American, too.

Relieved, Nori picked up the yellow flowers again. This time her hands seemed to fly as she placed them in the bowl. She arranged them with love.

Then she stood back to see the result. It looked natural—almost as if the sprays had grown right out of the bowl. It was beautiful and right.

That night, Nori put on the silk kimono her grandmother had given her. It was as blue as the sky with peach blossoms scattered across it. The long flowing sleeves fell almost to the floor.

Sometimes that evening Nori's steps were not as tiny as they should have been. But most of the time she remembered how to walk, and she knew she looked right most of the time. She, too, helped make the passing moments of that evening beautiful.

Grandmother said nothing about the flowers or the kimono. But Nori saw the glow of pride in her grandmother's eyes. She felt Grandmother's love reach out and wrap her like a cloak.

Outside, the wind blew through the cherry trees, scattering the white blossoms like snow against the moon.

ACTIVITY 1

Fact Questions

It is important to grasp the facts in a story. These questions will help you find out how well you grasp facts. Try to give your answer without looking back at the story. Write on your own paper.

1. Why did Nori say "I give up!"?
2. Who was Keiko?
3. Why did Keiko say Nori was lucky?
4. What did Nori want most of all?
5. What do the shortest flowers in a Japanese flower arrangement represent? The tallest? The medium size?
6. Why didn't Nori want to wear a kimono?
7. Why did Nori run into the garden and cry?
8. Name three things Nori saw in the garden.
9. What did Nori wear to the party?
10. Why did Nori have to walk carefully at the party?

ACTIVITY 2 — Thought Questions

Not all the meanings in a story are stated clearly in words. Sometimes you have to think about what you read. As you do, you find many additional meanings and much more enjoyment.

The answers to these questions are not stated clearly in the story. You have to think to find the answer. Write your answers on your own paper.

1. During what season of the year does the story take place?

2. Why do you think Nori had so much trouble arranging flowers?

3. What do you think Nori learned in the garden?

4. Why did Nori have no trouble arranging the flowers the last time she tried?

5. Why did Nori decide to wear the kimono after all?

6. Why do you think grandmother said nothing about the burned rice?

7. What customs or habits of the Japanese were difficult for Nori to learn?

8. What American customs or habits of Nori's might disturb or puzzle the Japanese?

ACTIVITY 3 — Understanding Setting in a Story

The following are characteristics, habits, or customs that might be found anywhere in the world. However, some of them are more likely to be Japanese and some are more likely to be American. On your paper, write *J* and after it the numbers of those customs that belong to Japan. Write *US* and after it the numbers of those customs more likely found in the United States.

1. taking shoes off before entering the house

2. doing as many tasks as possible in the shortest time

3. using three different lengths of flowers for flower arrangements

4. celebrating Thanksgiving with turkey

5. not questioning the decisions of the father of a family

6. wearing a kimono to a party

7. stopping work to look at the moon or a flower

8. never shouting in daily conversation

9. letting feelings, such as anger, show by words or tone of voice

10. wasting food

HOW TO READ IN SOCIAL STUDIES

The next selection is much like a reading you might find in a social studies book. In reading social studies, we pay close attention to the *causes* and *effects* of events. By learning why things happen as they do, we hope to manage our own future better.

A cause is anything which produces a result.

For instance, why did Jerry catch a cold? The *cause* of Jerry's cold may be exposure to Hal who coughed in Jerry's face. Without that exposure, Hal's cold may never have been transferred to Jerry. The *cause* is exposure to Hal's live germs. The result or *effect* is Jerry's runny nose, sore throat, and the other marks of a cold.

Often there is more than one cause for one event. For instance, lack of sleep and poor eating habits may have helped to cause Jerry's cold.

In the reading "Perry and the Opening of Japan," look for the causes of events. There may be more than one. Look for the results. Often there are many results or effects from one event, too.

Like Nori, we may learn things in unexpected ways. For instance, all these words have something in common: Datsun, Sony, Minolta, Toyota, Panasonic.

You have heard all these words in advertisements on TV, or you have seen them in newspapers and magazines. What do they have in common? They are all trade names of products made in Japan and sold around the globe. Because of products like these, Japan has become one of the world's most prosperous nations.

Yet it was not always so. Japan has become a world leader in a very short time—only a little more than a century. The United States was one of the causes of this change. Read to find out how we influenced a people so very different from us and so very far away.

Perry and the Opening of Japan

Written for this book
by Joseph H. Dempsey.

Until about 125 years ago, Japan kept to itself. No foreigners were allowed into Japan under penalty of death. No Japanese were allowed to leave. Japan was a hermit country.

It was the United States which forced Japan to abandon its hermit life. That action has had many results for Japan and the rest of the world. For Japan, it was one of the most important events in the nation's life story.

The Japanese felt that they had good reasons for shutting out the rest of the world. In the 16th century, missionaries from Portugal and Spain came to Japan. They persuaded thousands of Japanese to become Christians. Japan's

rulers saw this as a threat to their own power. So they forced the missionaries to leave, or had them killed. Christianity in Japan was wiped out.

For three centuries after that, Japan existed in isolation. The Japanese did not import any of the inventions which were changing the rest of the world. In 1850, Japanese soldiers were still using swords and bows and arrows. They knew of guns and cannons, but only as the weapons of Europeans who had come there about 300 years before.

The Japanese paid no attention to the rest of the world but they were being watched. People in other nations wanted to trade with Japan. As steamships began to replace sailing ships in the mid-1800's, trade with far-away countries was becoming easier. People in the U.S., particularly, wondered

---

Saburosuke Nakajima (sä boo rō′skə nä kä jē′mä)
Yokohama (yō kə hä′mə), seaport in Japan

43

what they might find in Japan. Our ships ventured closer and closer to Japan.

In 1853, the United States government decided on a bold move. It sent a fleet of ships to Japan to attempt to open the country for trade. The fleet was commanded by Commodore Matthew Perry. Commodore Perry was a stern and exceptionally able leader but he had a very difficult task. He was to lead a group of warships to a neutral country that did not want them. This could very well lead to war. Perry's orders were to make an agreement with Japan but to avoid any conflict.

Many people in the U.S. were critical of this mission. One New York newspaper said it was an invasion of Japan. Yet the feelings of most people at this time were that the U.S. had a duty to bring Western civilization to Japan. They felt that they had something special to give to Japan. They looked on Commodore Perry's mission as an act of charity.

Those who were against the mission felt that the real reason was to make money by opening trade with Japan. That did not seem to be a good enough reason for interfering in another nation's affairs.

Whatever the feelings at home, Perry had his orders. He knew that to deal with the Japanese he had to overcome obstacles of language, culture, suspicion, and ignorance on both sides. He prepared himself for the worst.

On July 8, 1853, Perry's fleet entered Tokyo Bay. The Japanese watching the ships were terrified. They had never seen steamships before. The ships were painted black, and black smoke billowed up from their stacks. They

steamed closer and closer. Some Japanese officials came out in small boats to stop them. They waved wildly, and some tried to board the ships. They were held back by bayonets. It began to look like an invasion. Instead, the U.S. ships anchored in the bay.

A vice-governor, Saburosuke Nakajima, was allowed on board. He was the first Japanese official ever to meet representatives of the American government.

Commodore Perry sent a young lieutenant to speak to Nakajima. Perry refused to speak himself, preferring to talk only with high officials of the Japanese Emperor. The lieutenant warned Nakajima to keep the Japanese boats away from the American ships. Nakajima, meanwhile, had noticed the size and number of guns on the American ship. He was impressed.

The lieutenant told Nakajima that Commodore Perry brought a letter from the U.S. President, Millard Fillmore, to the Emperor of Japan. The letter would not be given to the vice-governor but only to a higher ranking officer. Nakajima replied that the Americans could not stay in the bay but must sail south to another port.

Perry knew he had to prove he was strong and not afraid of the Japanese. At the same time, he had to convince them that he had come in peace and wanted only to be friends. He refused to move.

When Nakajima returned to shore, he told his superiors what the Americans wanted. The Japanese delayed. Each side tried to bluff the other. The Americans did not want war, but they did not move. The Japanese were unfriendly, but they did not attack.

Finally Commodore Perry received

45

permission to come ashore. He landed with 300 armed men, a band playing marching music, and many gifts for the Emperor.

The Japanese wanted time to think. They asked Perry to leave and to return in several months. Perry agreed and sailed out of the bay and south toward the China coast.

The following February, Perry returned with more ships. Anchored off the city of Yokohama in Tokyo Bay, the Americans waited for permission to come ashore. On March 8, 1854, Perry came ashore. With him were twenty-seven boatloads of men, three bands, and more gifts including a little steam locomotive complete with track.

As Commodore Perry arrived at the meeting place, the American ships sounded a 21-gun salute in honor of the Emperor. The Japanese were awe-struck. They promised to make a treaty of friendship. Then both Japanese and Americans enjoyed a ceremonial feast.

On March 31, 1854, the treaty was concluded. American citizens were protected on Japanese soil. Japan was opened to American trade and eventually to the world.

After that, the Japanese quickly learned what had been happening in the world closed off to them. Their swift progress was a marvel. In a short time, they became an industrial nation and a world power to rank with the strongest. Today Japan is one of the most influential nations of the world.

Two views of Commodore Matthew Perry

1
ACTIVITY

In understanding causes and effects, it is important to keep the time sequence clear in your mind. A cause must always happen before its effect.

On your paper, write the numbers of the following events in the order in which they happened. You are arranging them in time sequence.

1. Missionaries came to Japan in the 16th century.

2. On March 31, 1854, the first U.S.-Japanese treaty was made.

3. The U.S. sent a fleet commanded by Commodore Matthew Perry to open Japan to trade.

4. Japan became an industrial nation and a world power.

2
ACTIVITY

Read the unfinished statement and choose the best ending to complete it from the lettered choices which follow. On your paper, write the letter of the best ending next to the number of the statement.

1. Japan did not change very much for three centuries because
   a. Japan refused to let anyone in or out of the country.
   b. it learned Western ways very quickly.

2. Some people in the U.S. objected to Commodore Perry's mission to Japan because
   a. he would be bringing Western civilization to Japan.
   b. he would be interfering in another nation's affairs.

3. Commodore Perry refused to speak to the Japanese vice-governor because
   a. he preferred to talk with high officials of the Emperor.
   b. he did not speak Japanese.

4. The Japanese gave in to U.S. insistence and signed a treaty because
   a. they were afraid of what might happen to them if they did not sign.
   b. they were a powerful and influential nation in the world.

5. The sight of black steamships frightened the Japanese because
   a. Commodore Perry brought a letter from U.S. President Millard Fillmore to the Emperor.
   b. they had never seen steamships before.

HOW TO READ IN SCIENCE

This article is similar to material that you read in your science textbook. In science, a skill that you have to use often is that of drawing conclusions. In doing Activity 1 you will have practice in drawing conclusions. In Activity 2 you will have a chance to see how well you grasped facts.

1. First of all, preview the title, the diagrams, and the headings.

2. Read the article carefully, referring to the diagrams when you need to do so.

3. Do Activities 1 and 2.

After Japan was opened to the West, the Japanese had a whole new world to explore. An important part of this new world was the science and technology developed in the West. Modern medicine was one of these sciences. We are still learning more about the human body. This article tells about how our nerves and senses work together.

Your Nerves and Your Senses ___

Written for this book
by Maurice U. Ames.

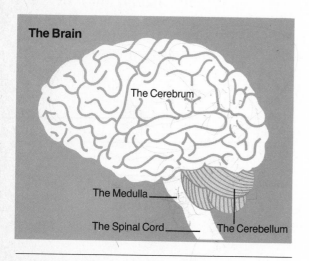

The Brain

The Cerebrum

The Medulla

The Spinal Cord

The Cerebellum

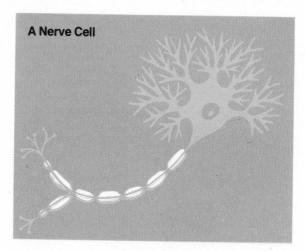

A Nerve Cell

---

cerebrum (ser′ə brəm), part of the brain which thinks and remembers

cerebellum (ser′ə bel′əm), part of the brain which controls posture, balance, and muscles

medulla (mə dul′ə), part of the brain which controls breath, digestion, and heart beat

reflexes (rē′fleks əz), automatic actions of the body

The Brain

Your brain is the most important part of your system of nerves. It is the most important organ of the body because it controls most of the body's activities.

The brain is divided into three main parts: the *cerebrum*, the *cerebellum*, and the *medulla*. A person thinks and remembers with the *cerebrum*. It makes up 85 percent of the weight of the brain. The size of the cerebrum in the human brain makes it very large as compared with the brains of other animals. However, mere size of a person's brain does not show how smart that person is.

The cerebrum of the brain has a covering. In this covering there are many grooves and ridges. This covering and part of the cerebrum itself are made up of grayish cells. These cells are called "gray matter." This gray matter is the "thinking" part of the brain.

The *cerebellum* is under the cerebrum. It controls posture and balance. It also controls the working together of different muscles. The cerebellum works automatically.

The *medulla* is somewhat below the center of the brain. It is also below the cerebrum. The medulla controls needed body actions, such as breathing, blood flow, and digestion of food. The medulla works even when the body is asleep or unconscious. An animal can breathe and live without a cerebrum or cerebellum. However, if the medulla is removed, the animal will quickly die. The medulla in the human brain is about the size of a walnut.

The Spinal Cord

The *spinal cord* is attached to the medulla. This cord is a long bundle of nerves. It is enclosed in the backbone, or spine. The spinal cord sends messages to the muscles for immediate actions. These instant actions are called *reflexes*. In a simple reflex action, the muscles move automatically before the message gets to the brain. For example, if you touch a hot iron, you quickly move your hand away. You move your hand before you really know what happened.

The spinal cord and the brain make up the *central nervous system* of the body. They are like a central telephone exchange. They receive and send messages from and to all parts of the body.

The Nerves

Nerves carry messages to and from the spinal cord and brain. They are made up of special cells called nerve cells. Nerve cells are found in the brain, spinal cord, and spinal nerves. They are also found in the organs we use to see, hear, smell, taste, and touch.

Nerve cells have long, string-like fibers to carry messages. They have branched ends to receive messages. Nerve cells are too small to be seen without a microscope. However, one thread from a nerve cell may stretch as much as three feet.

There are many kinds of nerve cells. The *sensory* nerve cells sense heat, light, sound, and pressure. They also sense chemicals connected with smells. *Motor* nerve cells carry messages from the brain or spinal cord to the muscles. They cause the muscles to move. *Connecting* nerve cells link the sensory nerve cells with the motor nerve cells.

Sensory nerve cells carry messages from the skin, muscles, and organs inside your body. Usually these messages go through the spinal cord to the brain. The brain then sends messages through the motor nerve cells to the muscles.

These different kinds of nerve cells enable us to hear, feel, see, taste, and smell.

The Senses

You have five main senses: touch, taste, smell, hearing, and sight. It is through these senses that you learn about the world in which you live. Many parts of your body have nerve cells that enable you to feel heat, cold, pressure, and pain.

Special sense organs, such as the skin, the tongue, the nose, the ear, and the eye have enabled human beings and animals to have the five important senses. These senses are not the same in all animals. Some animals have developed one sense more keenly than other animals have. Thus, a bloodhound has a much keener sense of smell than a human being. For this reason a bloodhound can follow the scent of a person when human beings are not aware of any scent at all.

1

ACTIVITY

See how well you can remember what you have just read. Try to answer the following questions without looking back at the article. Write your answers on your own paper.

1. Which part of the brain does one use to think and remember? Is it the cerebrum, cerebellum, or the medulla?

2. Which part of the brain controls posture, balance, and the working together of the body's muscles?

3. Which part of the brain controls such necessary body actions as breathing and blood flow?

4. What is "gray matter"?

5. What makes up the central nervous system of the body?

6. What does the spinal cord do?

7. What is a *reflex* action?

8. What do *sensory* nerve cells do?

9. What do *motor* nerve cells do?

10. Name the five senses.

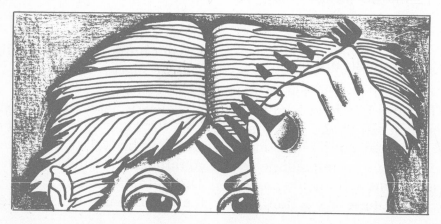

ACTIVITY 2

Each of the paragraphs below tells about something that happened to a person or animal. In every case, whatever happened had something to do with one of the senses. Read each paragraph and draw your own conclusion, based on what you have learned in this article. Write your conclusion on your own paper after the number of the paragraph.

1. Mr. Keller was injured in an automobile accident. Afterwards he could not think or remember anything about the life he led before the accident. What part of his brain was damaged?

2. Mr. Judd was in an accident. One of his arms became paralyzed. He could not move it. In the winter, however, he had to wear a mitten on the hand of the paralyzed arm. His hand could still feel heat, cold, or pain. What type of nerve cell was damaged?

3. A fire developed in a certain house one night. The rooms were filled with smoke. The people sleeping in the house were not aware of the odor of smoke. Their dog began barking loudly and woke them up. What do you think this shows about a dog's sense of smell?

4. Is it possible that some animals have an "odor language"? It was learned recently that some worker ants release certain chemicals to give a direction to other ants. These chemicals changed the behavior of the other ants. What is your conclusion about an "odor language" in ants?

5. Tom held a piece of apple and a piece of onion hidden in his hand. He told Bill to hold his nose and close his eyes. He then placed the piece of apple on Bill's tongue. Bill couldn't tell what it was. Next he placed the piece of onion on his tongue. Bill couldn't tell what it was. Tom then told Bill not to hold his nose. Bill could then tell the apple from the onion. Which sense in human beings is keener, taste or smell?

6. The school nurse had an instrument for use in testing hearing. Dick went to have his hearing checked. It happened that his dog went with him. Dick could hear up to as high a pitch as most human beings hear. After the nurse finished testing Dick's hearing, she turned the instrument to a higher pitch than Dick was able to hear. The dog "pricked up" his ears, and stood up and looked at the instrument. Which had the keener hearing, Dick or his dog?

In mathematics some words have new and different meanings. For example, in our ordinary conversation, when we say "a line," we may be talking about a straight line or a curved line. But in mathematics, "line" means a straight line only. And, strangely enough, in mathematics a "curve" may be made of straight lines.

We know that the Japanese were traditionally sensitive to lines and curves because of their art. But *line* and *curve* had new meanings in Western mathematics. Are you sure you know the meaning of *line*? Read this article to find out.

Lines and Curves _____

Written for this book
by William L. Schaaf.

Point

In mathematics ordinary words have new meanings. For instance, in mathematics, a point is not the end of your pencil or pen. A *point* is a location in space. A point is an idea; it is imaginary. We cannot see a point, but we can draw a picture of a point.

Here is a picture of point A.

.●A

The dot on the page shows the location, or place, of A on this page. It names this location.

1. Draw a picture of another point on your paper. Label it B.

Curve

A *curve* is the path between two points, or the path starting from and returning to the same point. The path may be straight or curved. It may loop around, zig-zag back and forth, or double back on itself. In fact, it is impossi-

ble to count the kinds of paths it would be possible to take.

On your own paper, you may draw a few of the many possible paths, or *curves*, between two points.

2. Draw two points on your paper. Label them C and D. Draw a zig-zag path between C and D.

3. Draw a looped path between points labeled E and F on your paper.

4. Draw the shortest path between two points labeled G and H.

If a curve starts at one point and ends at a different point, we call it an *open curve*. These are open curves. They have two end points.

If a curve starts at one point and ends at the same point, we call it a *closed curve*. These are closed curves.

ACTIVITY 1

On your own paper after each number, write *open* if the curve is open. Write *closed* if it is closed.

If a closed curve starts and returns to the same point without crossing itself, we call it a *simple closed curve*. Simple closed curves have only one interior (inside part). These are diagrams of simple closed curves.

The closed curves shown below are not simple because they cross themselves. They have more than one interior or inside part.

ACTIVITY 2

Study the curves shown here. Some of the curves are open, and some are closed. On your paper, write *open* or *closed* after the number of each curve. If a closed curve is a simple closed curve, write the word *simple* after the word *closed*.

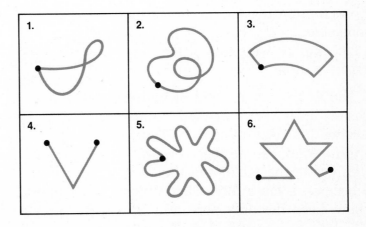

Finding the Main Idea in Different Places in Paragraphs

Usually the main idea is found in the first sentence of a paragraph. But this is not always true. Sometimes the most important thought comes at the very end of a paragraph. Sometimes it comes in the middle of a paragraph. In fact, the main idea may be in any part of a paragraph. To find it, you have to think about *all* the sentences. You have to decide which sentence sums up or includes all of the other sentences.

In the article below you will be asked to find the main idea in each paragraph. You won't find the main idea in the first sentence in all of these paragraphs.

Read all of the sentences in each of the paragraphs. Then decide which sentence is really most important. Find that sentence in the list of sentences beneath the paragraph. Write the letter of that sentence after the number of the paragraph on your paper.

Knives, Forks, and Spoons

Have you heard the old saying: "Fingers were made before forks"? This certainly is true. We have not always had knives, forks, and spoons. This story will tell you how we happened to have these tools.

1. Early in our history, people used knives for hunting and for protecting themselves. In fact, knives were one of the very first inventions. Knives made of flint were used in the Stone Age. In later years knives of bronze and iron were used by several different groups of people.

a. Knives made of flint were used in the Stone Age.

b. Early in our history, people used knives for hunting and for protecting themselves.

c. In fact, knives were one of the very first inventions.

2. The English were fond of boiled or roasted meat. They needed knives for carving this meat into slices. During the Middle Ages, people began bringing their knives to the table, and thus the knife became a table tool. The carver may have been the only person at the table with a knife. He or she cut the meat for the others. They ate it with their fingers.

a. The English were fond of boiled or roasted meat.

b. They ate it with their fingers.

c. During the Middle Ages, people began bringing their knives to the table, and thus the knife became a table tool.

3. The knife was not the only one of the table tools that was made early in history. Spoons also have been in use for thousands of years. A sign of how old spoons are is the word *spoon* itself. It comes from an Old English word that means "wood splinter," because the early spoons were made of wood.

a. The knife was not the only one of the table tools that was made early in history.

b. Spoons also have been in use for

thousands of years.

c. It comes from an Old English word that means "wood splinter," because the early spoons were made of wood.

4. In museums one often sees spoons that have been found in tombs of the Egyptians. These spoons are made of wood, stone, and ivory. The Greeks made spoons of bronze and silver. In the Middle Ages people used spoons made of bone, wood, and tin. Many different peoples used spoons made of various materials.

a. In museums one often sees spoons that have been found in tombs of the Egyptians.

b. The Greeks made spoons of bronze and silver.

c. Many different peoples used spoons made of various materials.

5. So it seems that people have used spoons and knives for a long time. Forks were used in other places long before they came to England. The dining fork was brought to England in 1608 by a traveler. The traveler had seen forks in Italy, where they had been used for many years. In a story of the eleventh century, the wife of a ruler was said to have used a fork in Venice. According to the story, this lady did not eat with her fingers. Instead, she had her food cut into little pieces and she ate it with a two-tined fork.

a. So it seems that people have used spoons and knives for a long time.

b. Forks were used in other places long before they came to England.

c. The traveler had seen forks in Italy, where they had been used for many years.

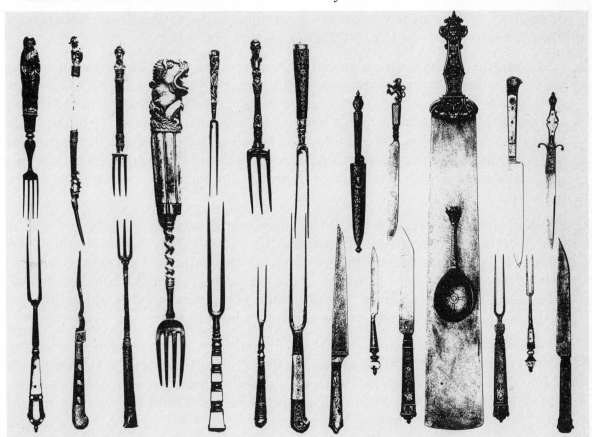

More Practice in Finding Main Ideas _____

It takes a lot of practice to become really skillful in finding main ideas in paragraphs. In the preceding exercise, three ideas were listed from each paragraph. You chose the one that was the main idea. In this lesson, the ideas are not listed for you. You will have to find the main idea within each paragraph. It will be one of the numbered sentences.

Read the following article. As you read each paragraph, look for a sentence which includes the ideas of the other sentences. The sentence which sums up the paragraph is the main idea sentence. Some of the other sentences are only examples or illustrations of the main idea sentence.

Write the number of the main idea sentence on your paper next to the letter of the paragraph.

A. (1) The Middle Ages were a colorful and romantic period in history. (2) This was the time in which lords and nobles lived in castles. (3) It was the period in which knights wore armor and rode beautiful horses. (4) This period inspired books, poems, and pictures. (5) It was a time that appeals to our love of adventure.

B. (1) We think of a castle as being a large, elegant house. (2) Castles, however, were not built to serve as beautiful homes. (3) Castles were mainly needed as fortresses. (4) There was continuous warfare at this time in history. (5) One lord often tried to take over the estate of another lord. (6) Bands of robbers and thieves overran the country. (7) People needed protection.

C. (1) The castle was built on a high hill whenever possible. (2) This was not so that the lord could have a pleasant view of the scenery. (3) It was so that the lord or his servants could see a warlike group coming to attack them. (4) The castle was a huge building, but not because the lord wanted many rooms. (5) It had to be large in order to house the knights who were needed to defend the castle. (6) Many farmers and their families also fled to the castle when enemies came near. (7) Castles were built high and large to protect the lord and the working people on his land.

D. (1) Was it fun to live in a castle? (2) The castle was not well heated. (3) A fireplace was the only means of providing warmth. (4) The walls were thick and damp. (5) The windows were narrow slits. (6) Very little sunlight reached the inside of the rooms. (7) For furniture, there were wooden stools, benches, tables, and chests. (8) The furniture was not made for comfort as it is today. (9) The castle really was an uncomfortable place in which to live.

E. (1) A boy began to train to be a knight at an early age. (2) At the age of seven, he was taken to the castle. (3) He served the lord and lady as page. (4) He went with them wherever they went. (5) He was supposed to learn good manners and loyalty. (6) His parents may have missed him at home. (7) But they were proud of him and felt he would have a bright future.

F. (1) At fourteen, a page was given the title of *squire*. (2) As a squire, the boy now was really learning what it was to be a knight. (3) He now began to serve one special knight. (4) He polished his knight's sword. (5) He waited on his knight at the table. (6) He went with his knight in time of battle. (7) If his knight were wounded or killed while fighting, the squire took his body away from the battlefield. (8) He watched a real knight and practiced his skills of swordsmanship and horsemanship.

G. (1) At the age of twenty-one, a squire who was chosen to be a knight went through a long ceremony. (2) Just before the ceremony, he prayed all night in church. (3) On the next day, nobles and ladies gathered in the courtyard. (4) As they looked on, his armor was buckled. (5) His sword was fastened at his waist. (6) Spurs were attached to the heels of his boots. (7) He then knelt before the lord or knight in charge of the ceremony to receive his salute. (8) This salute was given in a strange way. (9) The lord usually would hit the new knight three times on the shoulder with the flat side of a sword. (10) He then said a few words to the new knight about a knight's duties.

Reviewing Blends

You know that two consonants are sometimes blended together to make one sound. You know that such a sound is called a *blend*. But, are you sure that you know all of these sounds?

bl, cl, fl, gl, pl, sl   br, cr, dr, fr, gr, pr, tr
sc, sk, sm, sn, sp, sq, st, sw, tw

Look at these pictures. Pronounce the word that each of the pictures represents. What blend completes the word under the picture?

On your paper, write the number in the box. Next write the complete word that names the picture. Now underline the blend that begins each word.

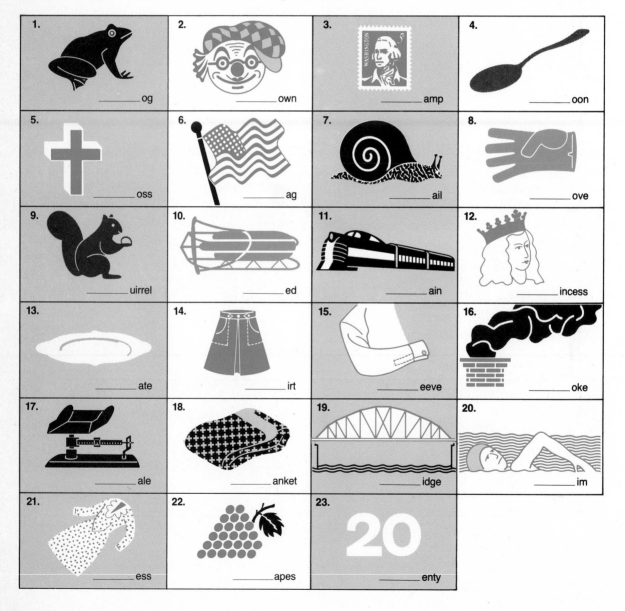

1. _____og

2. _____own

3. _____amp

4. _____oon

5. _____oss

6. _____ag

7. _____ail

8. _____ove

9. _____uirrel

10. _____ed

11. _____ain

12. _____incess

13. _____ate

14. _____irt

15. _____eeve

16. _____oke

17. _____ale

18. _____anket

19. _____idge

20. _____im

21. _____ess

22. _____apes

23. _____enty

Supplying Two-Letter Blends in Sentences _____

Here is an interesting article on bats. The words in some of the sentences are not complete. You will need to add a blend at the beginning of each of these words.

The words you will need are at the bottom of the page. Find the right word to use in place of each word that has missing letters. On your paper, write the number before each word with missing letters. Next to the number, write the complete word. Underline the blend, which is the part that was missing. For example, the first word is <u>bl</u>ind. You will need to use some words more than once.

You will need to use all of these blends:

bl, cl, fl, gl, pl   br, cr, dr, fr, pr, tr
sh, sk, sm, sp   tw

Do Bats Have a Sixth Sense?

Some people think that bats have a sixth sense. They are nearly (1) ____ind. But when they chase an insect, they (2) ____im about between (3) ____ees without (4) ____ushing against a single (5) ____anch or (6) ____ig.

A scientist caught a bat and (7) ____aced it in a (8) ____osed room. He then (9) ____ued something over the bat's eyes. The bat (10) ____ew about at a high (11) ____eed. It did not touch a picture (12) ____ame, a (13) ____ock, or furniture of any kind. It didn't even seem to be (14) ____ightened. This (15) ____oved that the bat did not depend on its eyes to keep from bumping into things.

The scientist then (16) ____osed its ears and mouth in the same way. The bat (17) ____undered about and then (18) ____opped to the (19) ____oor. As the bat (20) ____ies, it cries continuously. The scientist decided that the sound waves from the (21) ____ies hit any object in the bat's path and echo back. The bat hears this echo and is guided in the right direction.

There are many kinds of bats. The (22) ____all (23) ____own bats and the red bats are most common. The red bat, with (24) ____uffy red fur, is very pretty.

blind	clock	flies	glued	small
blundered	closed	floor	placed	speed
branch	cries	fluffy	proved	trees
brown	dropped	frame	shut	twig
brushing	flew	frightened	skim	

More About Blends

A. Some blends come at the *end* of a word instead of at the beginning.

Say these words softly to yourself and listen to the sound of the two consonants that blend at the end of each word. On your own paper, write the blends that you hear at the end of each word.

1. sing   **2.** land   **3.** went   **4.** stump   **5.** sink

See how well you can recognize blend sounds at the end of words. On your paper, write a blend to complete the word for each of the pictures below.

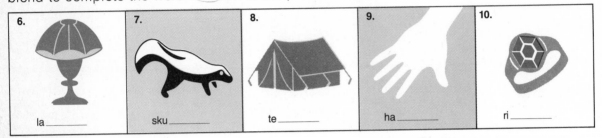

| 6. la_____ | 7. sku_____ | 8. te_____ | 9. ha_____ | 10. ri_____ |

B. Underlining blends

Read this article about whether birds have a sense of direction. On your paper, write the missing word for each numbered blank. Underline the blend at the end of each word. Here are the words you will need:

stamp   land   band   long   sent

A scientist caught several gulls. He put a (1)_____ around one leg of each gull. He had a (2)_____ with a date on it. He stamped the date on each band. Then he (3)_____ the birds to a faraway (4)_____, where they were set free. One morning the scientist heard, "Caw!" There were the banded gulls. It had not taken them a (5)_____ time to fly home. This helped to prove that birds have a sense of direction.

C. Some blends may come either at the end or the beginning of words.

1. Say these words: *sheep, push.* What blend comes at the beginning of *sheep?* Write the word on your paper and underline the blend. What blend comes at the end of *push?* Write the word on your paper and underline the blend.

2. Say these words: *chair, teach.* What blend comes at the beginning of *chair?* Write the word on your paper and underline the blend. What blend comes at the end of *teach?* Write the word on your paper and underline the blend.

3. Say these words: *think, bath.* What blend comes at the beginning of *think?* Write the word and underline the blend. What blend comes at the end of *bath?* Write the word; underline the blend.

4. What three blends may come either at the beginning or the end of words? Write them on your paper.

D. Some blends have two sounds.

1. Say: *thin, thing, these, thought.* In one of these words, the *th* sound is not the same as in the others. Write that word on your paper.

2. Say *wheat, who, white, whisper.* In one of these words, the *wh* sound is not the same as in the others. Write that word on your paper.

3. Make four columns on your paper. Give each column one of these four headings: *those, thin, whom, where.* From the following list, select those words with the same beginning sound as the heading and write them under it. There will be three words added to each column.

their	thick	thief	than	that	think
whale	who	whole	when	what	whose

E. Some words begin with three-letter blends.

Words beginning with three-letter blends often seem hard to pronounce. If you know the sounds of these blends you will have no trouble. These are some of the most common three-letter blends: *spr, str, shr, spl, scr, thr.*

Softly say the name that each of these pictures is supposed to stand for. As you say the name think about the sound of the beginning blend. The blend followed by the letters after the blank gives you the name of the picture. Write the whole word on your paper. Underline the blend.

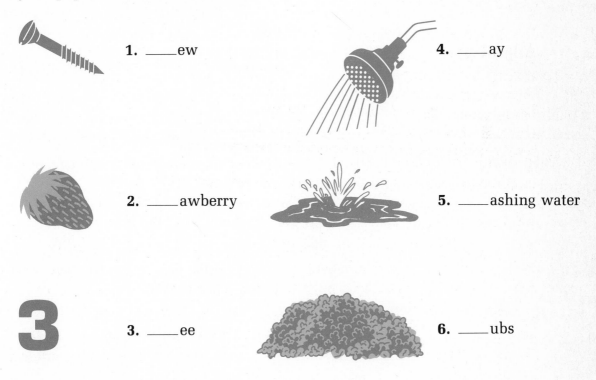

1. ____ew

2. ____awberry

3. ____ee

4. ____ay

5. ____ashing water

6. ____ubs

Reviewing Different Sounds of Vowels _____

A. Read the words to the right of each picture. Choose the one that names the picture. Write that word on your own paper. Answer the questions that follow.

1.    *plan* or *plane*?

2.    *not* or *note*?

3.   *cub* or *cube*?

4. Does each of the words that you wrote have a long vowel in it?
5. With what letter did each word end?
6. Is that letter silent or sounded?
7. Choose one of the words in the parentheses to complete this sentence. Write it on your paper.

Guide 1. When a word contains two vowels, one of which is final silent *e*, the first vowel is usually (long, short).

B. Read the words to the right of each picture. Choose the one that names the picture. Write this word on your own paper. Answer the questions that follow.

1.   *cot* or *coat*?

2.    *ran* or *rain*?

3.    *met* or *meat*?

4. Does each of the words that you wrote have two vowels together?
5. Was one vowel long and one silent?
6. Which vowel was long, the first or second?
7. Which vowel was silent?
8. Choose one of the words in parentheses to complete this sentence. Write it on your paper.

Guide 2. When two vowels come together in a one-syllable word you usually hear the (long, short) sound of the first vowel while the second vowel is silent.

C. Softly say the words below. Listen to the sound of each vowel when followed by *r*. Answer the questions that follow.

at, ate, art	gentle, gee, germ	gift, guide, girl
stand, state, star	fell, fee, fern	fist, file, first
can, cane, cart	tell, team, term	ditch, dike, dirt

cot, coat, corn	tub, tube, turn
hot, hope, horn	cub, cube, curl
not, note, nor	but, butte, burr

1. Do vowels followed by *r* have a sound which is neither long nor short?
2. Choose the word or words in parentheses that best complete the sentence.

Guide 3. If a sounded vowel in a word is followed by *r*, the sound of the vowel is usually changed by the *r*, and it is (short, long, neither short nor long).

Finding Different Vowel Sounds in Sentences

Some of the words in the story below are numbered and underlined. Look at the underlined words and do one of these things:

  1. If the vowel is long because of final *e*, write *1* after the number on your own paper.
  2. If the vowel is long because of two vowels together, write *2*.
  3. If the vowel has a changed sound because *r* follows it, write *3*.

On (1) her (2) first day in Japan, Terry was invited to a Japanese (3) home for dinner. Everyone in the Japanese family (4) came to the door and bowed in greeting. Terry bowed too, as low as she could. She knew that the lower she bowed, the (5) more respect she showed. She left her shoes at the door. In Japan, it is not polite to wear shoes inside.

Terry and her friends sat on mats on the floor. A (6) maid brought them (7) each a cup of (8) tea and a tray. On each tray was a small bowl of (9) rice and a larger bowl (10) for the (11) main course. It was a mixture of (12) meat and vegetables. It looked almost too good to (13) eat, but the (14) taste was even better. They used chopsticks, but they gave Terry a (15) fork.

When it was (16) time to go, the family went to the door with Terry and bowed again. Terry tried to bow even lower this time to show her thanks for the (17) fine (18) meal. She could see that to (19) serve a meal in Japan was an (20) art.

Dividing Words into Syllables

You are now meeting many long words in your reading. At first some of these words may seem hard to pronounce. They will be easy, however, if you divide them into syllables.

A syllable is a word or a part of a word having a sounded vowel. Silent vowels don't count. Answer the following questions on your paper.

1. How many sounded vowels are there in *step*?
2. How many syllables?
3. How many sounded vowels are in *trade*?
4. How many syllables?
5. Is the *e* in *trade* silent or sounded?
6. How many sounded vowels in *boat*?
7. How many syllables?
8. Is the *a* in *boat* silent or sounded?
9. How many sounded vowels in *merchant*?
10. How many syllables?
11. Are there any silent vowels?
12. How many sounded vowels in *airplane*?
13. How many syllables?
14. Which vowels are silent?
15. Choose one of the words in the parentheses to complete this sentence:

In every word, there are as many syllables as there are sounded (vowels, consonants).

■ Guide to Dividing Compound Words

Divide a compound word between the two words that make up the word as a whole. Divide each of the words below into syllables. Write it as two words on your paper. The answer to #1 is *week day*.

1. weekday	**3.** seaweed	**5.** driftwood
2. withdraw	**4.** flashlight	**6.** grassland

Working with Accent Marks

When pronouncing a word of two or more syllables, we *accent* one of them. We say one with more force than the others. An accent mark is used to show which syllable is said with more force. The accent mark looks like this ′. Here is a word broken into syllables and accented:

en joy′

Below are some words that you probably know. These words have been divided into syllables for you. On your paper, write the words broken into syllables.

Say each of these words softly to yourself. Then place an accent mark after the syllable that you say more forcefully. The first one is marked for you.

1. peo′ple	**8.** ca nal	**15.** at tack
2. pic ture	**9.** peace ful	**16.** kitch en
3. hap pen	**10.** em pire	**17.** con tain
4. riv er	**11.** fer tile	**18.** na ture
5. u nite	**12.** hu man	**19.** nap kin
6. val ley	**13.** rob ber	**20.** blan ket
7. pow er	**14.** doz en	**21.** fig ure

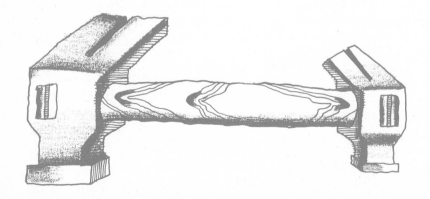

64

Working with Social Studies Words

The words below appear in social studies, history, and geography books at your grade level. You will be able to study your lessons in these subjects much better if you know the meanings and pronunciations of these words. Perhaps you think you can pronounce each one correctly, and that you know the special meaning of each word as it is used in these subjects. Do the work carefully anyhow—just to make sure.

Study the pronunciation of each word. Say the word to yourself. Then read and think about its meaning.

Arab (ar′əb), a native of Arabia or a person whose ancestors lived in the Arabian peninsula

citizen (sit′ə z′n), a person who by birth or choice is a member of a state or nation which gives certain rights and claims loyalty

communication (kə mū′nə kā′shən), the giving of information or news by speaking, writing, or printing words and symbols

delta (del′tə), a deposit of earth at the mouth of some rivers, usually a three-sided deposit of earth

nation (nā′shən), a group of united people who share a territory or a certain government

plateau (pla tō′), a plain of flat or rolling land above sea level

primitive (prim′ə tiv), living long ago in human history; or, like those living long ago

revolution (rev′ə loo′shən), a complete change in government, usually brought about by the people living under that government

tribe (trīb), a group of related families

See how well you understand the meaning of each of the words you have been studying. On your paper, write each sentence with the blank filled in. Put the right ending on the word to fit the sentence.

1. At the mouth of the Nile River soil and sand have been deposited in the shape of a triangle. This is a _____.

2. Newspapers, radio, television, magazines, and letters are all used as means of _____.

3. Knives made of stone were probably used by _____ people.

4. The only real _____ are those people born in Arabia or those whose ancestors lived in Arabia.

5. All people of Great Britain live under one government. This whole country can be called a _____.

6. Are you proud to be a _____ of the United States?

7. In ancient times there were many different _____ of people.

8. Our government was changed from English rule to a democracy after we had a _____.

9. Laramie, Wyoming, in the northwestern part of our country, is on a high plain which we call a _____.

Working with Science Words _____

The words below are found in science textbooks at your level. Make sure that you can pronounce each of the words correctly and that you know what each one means as it is used in science. Even if you think you know many of the words already, do the work just the same to make sure.

Study the pronunciation of each of these words. Say the word to yourself. Then carefully read the meaning of the word.

---

atmosphere (at′məs fêr), all the layers of gases which surround the earth and some of the other planets

atom (at′əm), the smallest particle into which an element can be divided and still have all the features of that element

calcium (kal′sē əm), a silver-white element that combines with other elements in chalk, limestone, sea shells, and the bones of human beings and animals

element (el′ə mənt), one of about 103 basic substances (such as oxygen, hydrogen, calcium, mercury, or gold) that does not contain any ingredients other than itself

energy (en′êr jē), the ability to do work or the power that does work, such as making things move

generator (jen′ə rā′tēr), machine that can change mechanical energy to electrical energy

hydroelectric power (hī′drō i lek′trik), electricity obtained by using the power of fast-flowing streams and waterfalls

turbine (tūr′bin), an engine, usually run by water power, which produces mechanical energy

---

See how well you know the meanings of the science words defined above. On your paper, write each sentence with the blank filled in. Put the right ending on the word to fit the sentence.

1. A jet flies high in the _____.

2. If a scientist could divide a piece of gold into the tiniest possible particles of gold dust, these particles would be called _____.

3. In the shells of water animals there is one layer made up mostly of limestone. Carbon is one element of this limestone. What do you think the other may be? _____

4. Although chemists can *add* different ingredients to a piece of gold, they cannot *divide* pure gold into different ingredients. Gold is an _____.

5. A town built near rapid falls in a strong river has a good chance of producing _____.

6. In the electric power plant in such a town, they would probably have an engine called a _____.

7. In this electric power plant, they would also need a machine to change mechanical energy into electric energy. This machine is called a _____.

8. Steam power can make a boat move or drive a train along a track. This power is one kind of _____.

3

Africa— Land of Contrasts

HOW TO READ LITERATURE

Practically every story has a *conflict* in it. The conflict is some kind of struggle or clash. The conflict makes us keep on reading to find out how the struggle comes out.

A conflict can be easily seen when it is between two people. Then it is like watching a fight. We read to see which person will win. It need not be an open fight. We could be watching one person trying to trick or outwit another person.

Conflicts are not only between people. They can be between a person and something outside—a force or a trend, a fact or an event. A scientist who is struggling to find a cure, for instance, is fighting against something —perhaps ignorance, perhaps a deadly disease. A farmer trying to raise a crop may be struggling against bad weather or insects.

Perhaps the most interesting kind of conflict is one that goes on inside a person. For instance, a young person may want to be more independent of his or her parents and at the same time may expect them to help out if it's necessary. So the young person may have a conflict of feelings. He or she may want help and at the same time want to be independent. This conflict goes on inside. It may not show on the outside, or it may show in peculiar ways, such as an outburst of anger or tears.

Struggle and conflict are a part of every life. Some conflicts are small and amusing. Some are important. You may be a part of some kind of conflict right now.

As you read "The Kom Thing," think about the kind of conflict in the story. Is it a conflict between two people? Is it a struggle going on inside one person? Or is it another kind of conflict?

Did you ever lose something important to you? Can you remember how you felt when you discovered your loss? What did you do to get it back? What happens when a whole group of people loses something important to them? Read on to find out.

The Kom Thing

Written for this book, by Glenn Munson.

One dark night in 1966, a man slipped from shadow to shadow in a small village in Africa. He carried a light, rolled-up grass mat on his shoulder. He stepped so softly that no one in the sleeping village heard him pass by their grass-roofed huts.

In the shadow of the mud wall of the king's house, the man stood, holding his breath, listening. . . . But no one stirred. Even the dogs missed his silent approach.

The man looked across the clearing to a clay-and-bamboo shed. The king's treasures were kept there. It was unguarded.

Clutching his mat, the man glided across the clearing, opened a bamboo door, and slipped inside the shed. A few minutes later, the door opened again. The man came out and moved

Afo-A-Kom (ä fō ā′käm), the name of a statue

Laikom (lī′käm), a small village in Africa

Mbang (mbaŋ, pronounced as one syllable), in an African language, a word meaning *statue*

scepter (sep′tēr), a staff held by a ruler as a sign of authority

69

quickly away. He carried something in his mat. Safely passing the last cluster of huts, he turned onto a dirt path. It led into the high elephant grass surrounding the village.

The man then balanced the grass mat on his head. It was wrapped and tied around a long heavy object, completely hiding it. Anyone seeing him would suppose he was carrying a body to some village for burial. That was the way the dead were often carried in the high grasslands of Cameroon.

In a way the night thief had left death in the village behind him. For he had stolen the Afo-A-Kom, a statue which the Kom people said was their life. The people believed they would die without their "Kom Thing."

The "Kom Thing," the Afo-A-Kom, is a carved wooden figure of a man. In his hand he holds the scepter of power. On his head he wears a crown. His face is covered with hammered copper, and his body is covered with red-brown beads. The Kom say that each bead stands for a man captured and dragged away to be sold in the slave trade long ago.

The wooden statue, standing about five feet high, was carved more than a hundred years ago by a king who brought strength and peace to the Kom people. It was kept in Laikom, a tiny village where the Fon (king) and his ruling council live. Laikom is the highest point in the Kom kingdom—about 300 square miles of grass-covered mountains like frozen green waves. About 35,000 Kom live in this part of Cameroon.

The Afo-A-Kom came out of storage once a year and whenever a new Fon was crowned. The Kom say that the statue "is the heart of the Kom, the spirit of the nation. It holds us together." If anything should happen to the carving, they said, sickness and sadness would come to the tribe.

Then, on August 20, 1966, a guard found that the Afo-A-Kom was missing. A shock ran through the kingdom. Their beliefs began to come true. Neighbors quarrelled. People took one another's land. Work went undone. And then the Fon died.

Another man became Fon. When he tried to find the missing statue, he discovered that a son of the former Fon had stolen the carving. He said he had been put under a spell. He had carried the Afo-A-Kom to a place outside the village. There he gave it to two boys. They took it down the mountain and gave it to a man named Ibraihim. Ibraihim, a member of another tribe, was a buyer and seller of African art. Ibraihim took the Afo-A-Kom in a Land Rover to a city called Douala, 300 miles away.

What happened then? The police asked Ibraihim many questions but he told them nothing. The new Fon went all the way to Douala to look for the Afo-A-Kom. He knew how important the statue was to his people. But the "Kom Thing" had disappeared.

Two years passed. The Kom people had lost all hope of getting the Afo-A-Kom back. All this time they felt they had nothing to protect them from sickness and death.

One day in 1973, an American Peace Corps worker in the Cameroon opened some mail from home. In it was a leaflet telling about a show of African art at an American college. On the cover of the leaflet was a picture of the Afo-A-Kom! The Peace Corps worker

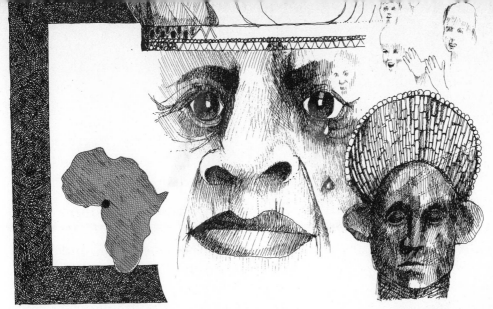

had heard about the statue from the Kom people. He wrote to the newspapers, telling them the story. The newspapers learned that the statue was indeed the Afo-A-Kom. It was owned by a man in New York who bought and sold African art.

"We must buy it back," said the Fon. "Everyone in the country will give money to bring the Afo-A-Kom back to us."

In the United States, many people read about the "Kom-Thing." A rich art collector and a big company joined to buy the Afo-A-Kom. They made plans for its 7,000 mile trip home. The statue would be packed in a crate. It would be flown to Africa strapped in a seat just like a passenger.

One day in early December, 1973, a truck drove through the twisting, dusty roads of Kom. Crowds lined the road. Women clapped their hands and made strange trilling sounds in their throats. Men danced through the high elephant grass, firing old muskets. In the larger villages, men and women and children crowded around the truck, hoping for a look at the crate that held their Afo-A-Kom. Throbbing drums spread the news that the "Kom Thing" was coming down the road.

When the truck at last pulled into Laikom, the Fon was on his throne, waiting for it. The crate was lifted from the truck and set gently on the ground. Hammers pulled at nails, freeing the top of the crate. Then workmen carefully lifted out the statue and stood it on the ground.

The Fon got up and walked slowly to the statue. He was more than 70 years old, but he stood tall and straight. He reached the carved statue and just looked at it for a moment. Then he ran his hands over the crown, the copper face, and the body covered with beads.

Thousands of Kom stood in the field, watching quietly. Then the Fon, with eyes wet with tears, said, "Welcome to our Mbang (statue). Welcome to the Afo-A-Kom." With that, the people rushed forward. Children were lifted onto their fathers' shoulders. "Mbang! Mbang!" they shouted.

For nearly a week, the Kom sang and feasted and danced. It was not such a long party—for people who had ended seven years of fear and sadness. The "Kom Thing" had come home.

It is important to grasp the clearly stated facts in a story. Try to answer these questions on your own paper without looking back at the story. If you have to, look back.

1. What is the Afo-A-Kom?

2. Where was the Afo-A-Kom kept?

3. About how many Kom people are there?

4. What kinds of houses do the Kom people have?

5. Who was the Fon?

6. Name three bad things that happened in the Kom kingdom after the theft of the Afo-A-Kom.

7. Who stole the Afo-A-Kom?

8. Who in Cameroon first found out where the Afo-A-Kom was?

9. Who bought the Afo-A-Kom and gave it to the Kom?

10. What is a Mbang?

2

ACTIVITY **Thought Questions**

Sometimes you have to think about what you read. As you do, you find many additional meanings and much more enjoyment.

The answers to these questions are not stated clearly in the story. You have to think to find the answer. Write your answers on your own paper.

1. Why do you think the Afo-A-Kom was not guarded?

2. Why do you think the thief took it?

3. Why was the Afo-A-Kom important to the Kom people?

4. How do you suppose the Fon found out who took it?

5. Why do you think the Fon could not find out more about the Afo-A-Kom in Douala?

6. If you were the Fon, what other things would you do to find the Afo-A-Kom?

7. Do you think the Kom people did all they could to find the Afo-A-Kom?

8. Why do you suppose Americans bought the Afo-A-Kom and gave it back to Kom?

9. Why do you think people like to have heirlooms, things inherited from their ancestors?

10. Why do you think the Afo-A-Kom was unharmed?

3

ACTIVITY

**Understanding
Conflict in a Story**

The main conflict in "The Kom Thing" was a struggle of the Kom people to find the Afo-A-Kom. It was a struggle between the people and an outside event that had happened unexpectedly. All through the story there were different situations or events that had to be resolved or decided. Each of these had an element of conflict.

Match the events in Column I with the question in Column II. On your paper, write the number of the event and the letter of the question that matches it. For example, the answer to 3 is A.

I

1. A thief creeps through the village.

2. The new Fon goes to Douala in search of the Afo-A-Kom.

3. A Peace Corps worker sees a picture of a statue like the Afo-A-Kom in an announcement of an art exhibit in the U.S.

4. Americans buy the Afo-A-Kom as a gift to the Kom.

5. The Fon dies and other bad things happen to the Kom.

II

A. Is the real Afo-A-Kom in the U.S.?

B. Will the Afo-A-Kom safely travel from the U.S. to Laikom?

C. Will the Fon find the Afo-A-Kom in Douala?

D. Will death now come to the Kom as they fear?

E. Will the villagers wake up and catch him?

HOW TO READ IN SOCIAL STUDIES

Reading to find contrasts and likenesses is a very important skill in social studies.

1. Preview the picture and headings.

2. Read the article carefully.

3. As you read, look for the main idea in each paragraph. It won't be at the *beginning* of a paragraph. You will have to search for it.

In the next article, each group of paragraphs under a heading will tell you about some kind of contrast. A *contrast* is a difference. The first paragraph under the heading tells you about one thing. The second tells you about something that contrasts with, or is different from, the first paragraph. The two paragraphs together add up to a contrast.

74

Sometimes we can understand a story very well because we have had somewhat similar experiences. For instance, we can understand the feelings of the Kom for their statue because of our own experiences. We might be very upset when our country's flag is mistreated.

Nevertheless, there is much about foreign peoples and places that we might not understand. It might seem strange to us to carry heavy things on our heads, and we cannot easily imagine living in a thatched hut.

In learning about foreign places, we see both similarities and differences. Notice the differences this selection points out about Africa.

Some Differences in Africa

Written for this book by Marius Livingston.

Contrast in Surface Features

The Sahara Desert in northern Africa is the largest desert in the world. It consists of drifting sand dunes, rocky uplands, and vast stretches of gravel. There are two smaller deserts in southern Africa. They, too, are sandy and barren. About two-fifths of Africa is dry, barren desert land.

Quite different from the desert are the grasslands and rain forests in central Africa. These lands reach out on both sides of the equator. The hot sun causes the air to rise. Moist air from the sea comes in. Heavy rains fall. Close to the equator where it is both very hot and damp, dense rain forests grow. On either side of the forests there are fields of tall, waving grass.

Contrast in Homes

Let us take a look at the homes of the poor. The homes of the poor farmers are often primitive. Many African farmers live in mud huts. The roofs are covered with straw or large leaves. Shepherds who travel from place to place live simply. Usually their homes are not much more than a tent-like covering made of wood and animal skins. In cities laborers often live in tar-paper shacks. The homes of many poor Africans are primitive and offer little in the way of modern comforts.

In the larger cities there are beautiful, modern buildings. Many people live in apartment houses that are up-to-date in every way. People living in these apartment houses have all of the

comforts of life. Other people who have good-paying jobs own modern and well-built houses. Some farmers own hundreds of acres of land and have attractive homes. It is clear, then, that many other people in Africa have comfortable, up-to-date homes.

Contrast in Industry

The U.S. and most European countries contrast greatly with Africa in the amount of manufacturing done. In the industrial countries of Europe and North America, most people live in cities. There they work in factories, shops, and offices. Of course, farmers are a part of the population, too. But the numbers of farmers are few. Many people work in some kind of manufacturing.

In Africa the amount of farming is great compared to the amount of manufacturing. Some Africans clear bushes and trees from a patch of ground. They farm this patch of ground as long as the ground is fertile. Then they move on and clear another patch of ground. Others live in villages in which the people of the village own the land together. Some large modern farms in Africa are owned by Europeans. Manufacturing is done in a few large cities.

Contrast in Population

Because of Africa's size, we might expect it to have a large population. Africa is the second largest continent in the world. (Eurasia is the largest continent.) Yet for the whole continent of Africa there are only 26 people per square mile. While Africa makes up almost one-fifth of the world's area, it has only about a twelfth of the world's population.

At present the United States has somewhat more than 55 people per square mile. In some states where there is a great deal of industry, the number of people per square mile is much higher. In New Jersey, for example, there are 950 people per square mile. North America supports nearly as many people as Africa on less land because of industrialization.

ACTIVITY 1

In the article, the main ideas of the paragraphs under each heading contrast with each other. Read the beginning of the sentences below and choose the best ending in order to make a contrast. The first part of each sentence is the main idea of one paragraph. The second part of the sentence is the main idea of the following paragraph. Write the number of the sentence and the letter of the best ending on your paper.

1. About two-fifths of Africa is dry, barren desert land, but
   a. quite different are the grasslands and rain forests in central Africa.
   b. the hot sun causes the air to rise.

2. The homes of many poor Africans are primitive and offer little in modern comforts, but
   a. some farmers own hundreds of acres of land and have attractive houses.
   b. many other people in Africa have comfortable, up-to-date homes.

3. In the industrial countries of Europe and North America, most people live in cities, while
   a. in Africa the amount of farming is great compared to the amount of manufacturing.
   b. some Africans clear bushes and trees from a patch of ground.

4. While Africa makes up almost one-fifth of the world's area, it has only about a twelfth of the world's population, but
   a. at present the U.S. has somewhat more than 55 people per square mile.
   b. North America supports nearly as many people as Africa on less land because of industrialization.

The article gives facts and information and describes the process of making hydroelectric power. You will read this article differently from the way you read a story.

The article and the diagram tell you the major steps in producing electricity in a hydroelectric power plant. The process is much the same in all parts of the world.

1. Study the diagram. Read the names of all the parts and follow the arrows to find the parts. Then try to name the parts without reading the names on the diagram.

2. Read each paragraph one sentence at a time. After you read each sentence, look at the diagram, find the parts of the machinery that are mentioned, and try to understand just what happens, as described in the sentence.

3. When you have finished reading each paragraph, look away from the book. Try to tell yourself just what happens in that particular step of the process. Check your recall by rereading the paragraph to see if you left anything out. If you did, try telling yourself the entire process again, including each step.

While many Africans are content with the traditional life, such as that lived in the village of Laikom, many others want change. They hope that using Africa's water resources may help bring about that change. Africa's many rivers can provide power for manufacturing if they are harnessed properly. How do you harness a river?

How a Hydroelectric Power Plant Works

penstock (pen′stok), a tube for controlling the flow of water

turbine (tūr′bin), an engine driven by the pressure of steam, water, or air against the blades of a wheel

generator (jen′ə rā tēr), a machine for changing mechanical energy into electrical energy

hydroelectric (hī drō i lek′trik), producing electricity by water

Water is carried from where it is stored behind the dam into the plant and out again through large tubes. These tubes are called penstocks. The penstocks are arranged so that the water will run downhill. This gives it still more pressure.

The water is directed to run through

a turbine. The turbine has blades something like a water wheel. When the water strikes the turbine blades, it travels at a very high speed. The water then turns the blades at a high speed.

A shaft leads from the turbine to the generator. As the turbine turns, the shaft turns. The shaft spins the generator.

The generator itself is made up of coils of copper wire and an iron core. As the generator spins, it causes a flow of current. It is in the generator that electricity is made.

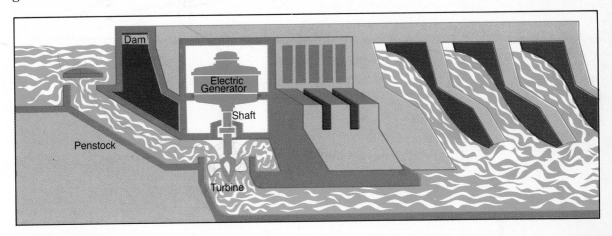

1 ACTIVITY

In Column I are the names of parts of a hydroelectric plant. In Column II are descriptions of what these parts do. On your paper, match the number of the part in Column I with the letter of the description of what it does in Column II.

I	II
1. dam	**A.** connects the turbine with the generator
2. penstock	**B.** stores water
3. generator	**C.** tubes for carrying water into the plant and out
4. shaft	**D.** catches the flowing water with its blades and turns swiftly
5. turbine	**E.** causes a flow of electric current

2 ACTIVITY

Reread the article carefully. As you read, look for the four major steps in producing electricity from water power. Write these four steps on your paper.

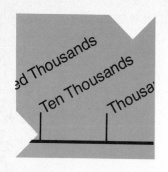

You may have noticed that you read the material in your mathematics books differently from the way you read a story. In this lesson, you will be reading and writing decimals in numbers and also in words.

You have seen and used decimals often. You probably have used a *decimal point* to write dollars and cents. Now you will *read* decimals, fractions, and decimal place values. Write the answers to the questions on your own paper.

Africa played a part in the way we write numbers. We are thought to have derived our numbers from the Arabs in North Africa and in Arabia.

Modern mathematics is a kind of international language which can be understood in every country. Yet each person has to translate the numbers into the words of his own language. How well can you read decimals? Find out in this article.

Reading Decimals

Written for this book
by William L. Schaaf.

A. Fractions and Decimals

Here are some fractions we can write as decimals without actually dividing.

$$\frac{5}{10} \qquad \frac{139}{10,000}$$

$$\frac{14}{100} \qquad \frac{88}{100,000}$$

$$\frac{6}{1,000} \qquad \frac{30}{1,000,000}$$

Look at the denominators of the fractions shown above.

1. These denominators may all be divided by

    a. 3   **b.** 10   **c.** 7

As you have discovered, a fraction which can be written as a decimal without dividing must have a denominator of ten or a power of ten. A power of ten means that ten is multiplied by ten, one or more times. For example, 100 is a power of ten, since $10 \times 10 = 100$. If the denominator is 10 or a power of 10, the fraction can be written as a decimal.

2. Can $\frac{5}{100}$ be written as a decimal?

3. Can $\frac{15}{1,000}$ be written as a decimal?

4. Can $\frac{137}{1,000}$ be written as a decimal?

Any fraction which has a denominator of ten may be written as a decimal. Table I shows how we would write these fractions as decimals and how we would read the decimals. Notice that the first place to the right of the decimal point is called *tenths*.

Table I

Fraction	Decimal	Read
$\frac{1}{10}$	.1	one tenth
$\frac{2}{10}$	.2	two tenths
$\frac{3}{10}$	.3	three tenths

On your own paper, write the following fractions as decimals. Then write the decimals in words. The answer to #5 is shown.

5. $\frac{5}{10}$ .5 *five tenths*
6. $\frac{4}{10}$
7. $\frac{7}{10}$

Any fraction which has a denominator of one hundred may be written as a decimal. Table II shows how we would write these fractions as decimals and how we would read the decimals. We use zero as a place holder for the tenths place.

Table II

Fraction	Decimal	Read
$\frac{1}{100}$	.01	one hundredth
$\frac{8}{100}$	.08	eight hundredths
$\frac{25}{100}$	.25	twenty-five hundredths

On your own paper, write the following fractions as decimals. Then write the decimals in words.

8. $\frac{5}{100}$
9. $\frac{26}{100}$
10. $\frac{32}{100}$
11. $\frac{3}{100}$

B. Place Value

Decimals have place value. This chart shows some of the names in our place value system.

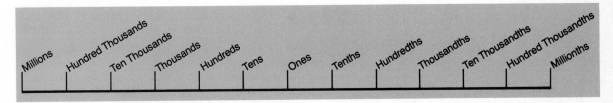

Look at the chart shown above. No matter where you start, as you move to the *left*, each place is worth ten times more than the place before it. (1) If we start from the ones place and move left, what is the name of the next place? This place is worth ten times as much as the ones place. (2) If we start in the hundredths place and move left, what is the name of the next place? This place is worth how many times as much as the hundredths place?

(3) Which place is worth ten times as much as the hundred thousands place?

(4) Which place is worth ten times as much as the thousands place?

As we move to the *right* in our place value system, each place is worth one-tenth of the place before it. (5) If we start with the hundreds place and move right, what is the name of the next place? This place is worth one-tenth as much as the hundreds.

Reading and Organizing Details

You have had practice in finding the main idea in paragraphs. In some cases finding these larger, basic ideas will serve your purpose. In much of your studying, however, you need to grasp and understand details. Reading for details can sometimes be more difficult than reading for main ideas. There are ways, however, of learning to grasp details easily and quickly.

The first step to take in finding details in a paragraph is to find the main idea. The smaller ideas grow out of the main idea. Once you get a "picture" of smaller ideas growing out of a main idea, it is easy to grasp these smaller ideas.

Diagraming a paragraph is helpful in getting a "picture" of a main idea and its details. You will now be shown how to diagram a paragraph. Read the paragraph below to see if you can find the main idea.

An African Family

Many Africans have ideas of family life that are different from ours. They do not think of a family as consisting only of father, mother, and children. An African family includes uncles, aunts, and grandparents. All members of this family often have one piece of land in common. Any member of a family has the right to ask food from another.

No doubt you discovered at once that the main idea is: *Many Africans have ideas of family life that are different from ours.*

Now find several details of about equal importance that tell more about this main idea. How many details did you find?

Think of this whole set of details together with the main idea as making one cluster of ideas. Perhaps the block diagram below will help you to "picture" the entire paragraph.

Many Africans have ideas of family life that are different from ours.			
They do not think of a family as consisting only of father, mother, and children.	An African family includes uncles, aunts, and grandparents.	All members of this family often have one piece of land in common.	Any member of the family has the right to ask food from another.

Finding and Blocking Off Major Details _____

Some additional paragraphs are given below. You are to make block diagrams of these paragraphs. You are given block forms for the first two paragraphs. Paragraph 1 has been filled in for you. Paragraph 2 has been partly filled in. On a separate sheet of paper make your own block diagrams for paragraphs 2, 3, and 4.

1. Some farming is done even in the deserts of Africa. This farming takes place near rivers or in oases. Desert farmers grow dates, cotton, and vegetables. Some of the farm products are traded or sold.

2. The ostrich is an unusual bird. It is the largest bird in the world. Strange to say, it cannot fly. It can run very fast.

3. The giraffe is one of Africa's most interesting animals. It is the tallest ani-

mal in the world. Its long neck enables it to reach leaves on trees. Its long legs give it a headstart in running away from enemies. The giraffe stands up while it sleeps.

4. Means of traveling are poorly developed in Africa. There are few paved roads. Most roads are of gravel. Waterfalls in many rivers prevent boat travel. In the rain forests, crews have to hack a path through the jungle.

Some farming is done even in the deserts of Africa.

This farming takes place near rivers or in oases.	Desert farmers grow dates, cotton, and vegetables.	Some of the farm products are traded or sold.

The ostrich is an unusual bird.

It is the largest bird in the world.		

Vowel Combinations _____

You have had some work in this book with two or three consonants which blend together to make one sound. Sometimes when two *vowels* appear together they make one sound. (*Y* is sometimes a vowel. It is a vowel in the sound made by *oy*.) Write the answers to the following questions on your own paper.

oy and *oi*

1. Say this word, listening for the sound of *oy*: *boy*. Do you hear the sound of *o* or the sound of *y*, or just one blended sound?
2. Say this word, listening for the sound of *oi*: *boil*. Did *o* and *i* have separate sounds or just one blended sound?
3. Did *oy* in *boy* and *oi* in *boil* sound alike or different?

ee and *oo*

4. Say this word: *deep*. Did you hear a sound for each *e* separately?
5. If you heard a sound for just one *e*, was it long or short?
6. Say these words and listen to the sound of *oo*: *school, soon, loop, book*. In one word, the sound of *oo* was different from the others. Which one was it?
7. Listen to the sound of double *o* in each of these words: *soon, good, moon, hood, school, noon, cook, brook*. On your paper, make two columns. Write *cool* at the head of one column and write *look* at the head of the other column. Write each word in the above list under the word with the same *oo* sound. There will be four words in each column.

aw, *al*, and *au*

8. Listen to the vowel sound in the first word of each of these groups. On your paper, write two other words in each group that have the same vowel sound as the first word.
   a. *lawn:* cane, tall, taught
   b. *hall:* straw, dear, cause
   c. *haul:* stall, stem, claw
   d. *crawl:* autumn, school, wall

One Vowel Sound for *a, e, i, o,* and *u* _____

Listen to the vowel sound in these words: *bus, mug, hum, tub, luck.* Sometimes any one of the vowels *a, e, i, o,* or *u* may have a very soft sound that is something like short *u* pronounced very lightly.

Write the answers to these questions on your paper.

1. Pronounce *ago.*   Which vowel sounds like a soft, short *u*?
2. Pronounce *taken.*   Which vowel sounds like a soft, short *u*?
3. Pronounce *evil.*   Which vowel sounds like a soft, short *u*?
4. Pronounce *season.*   Which vowel sounds like a soft, short *u*?
5. Pronounce *suppose.*   Which vowel sounds like the *u* in *bus*?
6. Finish the sentence: Sometimes *a, e, i, o,* and *u* may all sound like _____.

This sound which all vowels may have at times is called the *schwa* sound.

The words below have been divided into syllables. Copy them the same way on your paper. Say each word softly. Decide which vowel has the *schwa* sound. Underline that vowel. Then say the words again. Decide which syllable is accented in each word. Place the accent mark where it belongs.

Example: The answer to #7 is wag′on.

7. wag on	11. ap ply	15. ze bra	19. spo ken
8. a ware	12. gar ment	16. o ral	20. at tack
9. gal lop	13. pos si bly	17. ap pear	21. se rum
10. plur al	14. sup ply	18. gal lon	22. kitch en

23. Choose the right words in the parentheses to complete the sentence:

The *schwa* sound in the above words always falls in an (accented, unaccented) syllable.

(In the dictionary, the *schwa* sound is indicated by this symbol: ə.)

Reviewing the Two Sounds of *c* and *g* _____

The consonant *c* has two sounds. One sound is the hard sound as in *cave*. The other sound is the soft sound as in *cent*.

Say the name of each of the pictures below. Decide whether the word begins with hard *c* or soft *c*. Write "hard *c*" or "soft *c*" after each number on your paper.

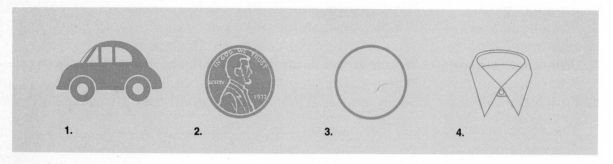

1.   **2.**   **3.**   **4.**

Two Sounds of *c*

Are you sometimes puzzled in deciding whether *c* has a hard or soft sound in a word? There are guides to help you. On your paper, write the vowel that follows the hard *c* in each group of words. Number your answers.

1. card, camel, candy, call

2. color, comb, coffee, cog

3. cup, custard, cucumber, cube

4. On your paper, finish this sentence: *C* is usually hard when followed by these three vowels: . . . .

Now write the vowel that follows the soft *c* in each of these groups:

5. cellar, central, cent, cedar

6. cider, city, circle, cinnamon

7. On your paper, finish this sentence: *C* is usually soft when followed by these two vowels: . . . .

Two Sounds of *g*

On your paper, write the vowel that follows the hard *g* in each of the groups below.

1. garden, gable, gain, gay

2. goose, goat, goal, goad

3. gum, gulf, guppy, gun

4. On your paper, finish this sentence: *G* is usually hard when followed by these three vowels: . . . .

Now write the vowel that follows the soft *g* in each of these groups:

5. germ, gentle, German, gesture

6. gypsy, gymnasium, ecology

7. On your paper, finish this sentence: *G* is usually soft when followed by the two vowels: . . . .

Noticing Sounds of c and g in Blends

If you notice whether or not c or g is a part of a consonant blend, you will have another guide.

On your paper, write the blend in each group in which c or g appears. Write *hard* or *soft* after each for the sound of the c or g.

1. clam, class, clank

2. crawl, credit, crab

3. glove, glass, glance

4. grope, ground, growl

5. Choose the best word in the parentheses to complete the sentence: When c or g is part of a blend with *l* or *r*, the sound of c or g is usually (hard, soft).

Completing Sentences

Choose the best word in the parentheses to complete the sentence.

1. The c in *cell* has the (hard, soft) sound because it is followed by (e, l).

2. The c in *coin* has the (hard, soft) sound because it is followed by (o, i).

3. The c in *clay* is (hard, soft) because it is part of the blend (cl, la)

4. The g in *gym* has the (hard, soft) sound because it is followed by (y, m).

5. The g in *gun* has the (hard, soft) sound because it is followed by (u, n).

African Riddle

The answer to a riddle is hidden below. Use the rules you have learned about the hard and soft sounds of c and g to find the answer. If the word has the hard sound of c or g, write on your paper the letter next to the word. If the c or g has a soft sound, do nothing. The letters you write on your paper will answer this question: What African animal eats with its tail?

1. graze —T	12. gym —A	23. civil —U	34. gray —T	45. camera —I
2. code —H	13. great —O	24. gum —N	35. German —R	46. cease —R
3. cereal —A	14. gun —T	25. circle —L	36. clear —H	47. crash —L
4. garden —E	15. citizen —A	26. good —T	37. cement —U	48. grape —S
5. cell —L	16. canal —H	27. ceiling —O	38. glue —E	49. glow —O
6. grassy —Y	17. center —O	28. cot —T	39. cook —I	50. city —V
7. coat —A	18. cart —E	29. gold —A	40. certain —V	51. gallop —F
8. cover —L	19. circus —S	30. gentle —P	41. gas —R	52. cedar —E
9. cellar —P	20. gap —Y	31. close —K	42. gang —T	53. general —R
10. gaze —L	21. catch —C	32. cigar —S	43. gem —H	54. cream —F
11. cross —D	22. cube —A	33. gain —E	44. gallon —A	

Working with Social Studies Words

The words below often appear in the social studies, history, and geography books used at your school level. You will be able to understand these subjects better if you know the meanings and pronunciations of these words. Perhaps you think that you can already say each word correctly and that you know the special meaning of each word as it is used in these subjects. Study the pronunciations and meanings below to be sure. Say the word to yourself. Then read and think about its meaning.

---

annual (an′yoo əl), coming once a year

cabinet (kab′ə nit), a group of people chosen by the head of a nation to advise him about affairs of government

commerce (kom′ērs), buying and selling in large amounts

community (kə mū′nə tē), people with common interests usually living in one area

cultivation (kul′tə vā′shən), preparing soil and caring for crops

export (eks′pôrt), sending goods out of one country for sale in another one

import (im′pôrt), bringing goods in to buy from a foreign country

industry (in′dəs trē), any branch of business, trade, or manufacture; as in "the steel industry"

poverty (pov′ēr tē), the condition of being poor; without much money

republic (ri pub′lik), a nation or state in which the citizens elect representatives who manage their government

---

See how well you understand the meaning of each of the words you have been studying. On your paper, write each sentence with the blank filled in.

1. Africa can _____ diamonds.

2. Africa must _____ machinery.

3. South America and the United States have products to exchange. They carry on _____ with one another.

4. In England, manufacturing is the chief _____.

5. All countries should try to get rid of _____ so their people may have a better life.

6. Many people in Africa live on a small piece of land and spend their time in the _____ of crops.

7. In the United States the people elect their senators and representatives to carry on affairs of government. Our nation is a _____.

8. Do you have a good school in your _____?

9. The Nile River has an _____ flood.

10. The President of the United States called a meeting of his _____ to help solve a problem.

Working with Mathematics Words

The words below appear in most mathematics books. You will be able to understand your lessons in mathematics better if you know the meanings and pronunciations of these words. Perhaps you think that you can already say each one correctly, and that you know the special meaning of each word as it is used in mathematics. Study the pronunciations and meanings below to be sure. Say the word to yourself. Then read and think about its meaning.

---

area (ãr′ē ə), amount of surface; extent

circumference (sẽr kum′fẽr əns), the distance around a circle

consecutive (kən sek′yoo tiv), following one another without a break in order; 10, · 11, and 12 are consecutive numbers

dimension (də men′shən), measurement of length, breadth, or thickness

equation (i kwā′zhən), an expression of two equal quantities, equally balanced, such as $(3 \times 6) + 4 = 22$

equivalent sets (i kwiv′ə lənt), two sets of objects that are exactly alike in number; such as △△△ ○○○

notation (nō tā′shən), a set of signs or symbols to represent numbers, quantities, and other values, such as 6, 7, 9, 20

perimeter (pə rim′ə tẽr), the distance around the outer boundary of a surface or figure

solution (sə loo′shən), the answer obtained by solving a problem

---

Copy the sentences below on your paper, filling in the blanks. In some sentences you are to fill in the space with one of the words you have just studied. You will have to add *s* to one of the words.

In other cases you will be asked to answer a question or to work with numerals. In one case you will be given directions for making a drawing.

1. Write consecutive numbers from 1 to 5. _____

2. Here is a circle. Which is the circumference, a, b, or c? _____

3. The _____ of Mr. Johnson's lot are 50 ft. by 72 ft.

4. Here is a rectangle. If you find the sum of the number of inches in the four sides you will know the sum of inches in its _____.

5. These are symbols from the Roman system of number _____: I, X, XXI.

6. Place the missing number in this expression: $(2 \times 4) + \square = 10$. What is such an expression called? _____

7. Draw equivalent sets. Show any objects you like in them.

8. The top of the dining room table in Bill's home contains 24 square feet. This is the _____ of the top.

9. Tom spent 50 cents and 20 cents. He spent _____ altogether. What is this answer called? _____

4

Sea Adventures

**HOW TO READ
LITERATURE**

Character is one of the most fascinating elements in fiction. *Character* means a person in a story, as when we say, "There were two main characters." *Character* also means the qualities that make a person what he is. We are using the word this way when we say, "His character was mean and grasping," or "Her character was generous and forgiving."

The characters in a story usually have a close connection with its conflict. What people do depends on what they are. In the next story, you will see that Spooner's actions are the result of the kind of person he is. Character may also be closely connected with setting. Time and place help mold a person. For instance, people in a small town may be more used to helping each other than people in a large city.

In this unit, we have a fiction story and a news story based on the same event. Notice the differences between the two. Does the news story tell you more or less than the fiction story? Does the news story have a purpose different from that of the fiction story? Are the facts the same in both? Enjoy the stories. After you have read them both, compare them, keeping these questions in mind.

Did you ever feel you had something important to say—and nobody paid any attention? Sometimes people don't listen because you are young or because they think you don't know enough. But sometimes you *do* know enough and it *is* important. That was the situation for Spooner in the next story. Read to see what he did about it.

The Dolphin Disaster

Written for this book
by Glenn Munson.

One foggy September day, the dolphins came to Port Hegen. Fishermen were setting their lobster traps in the waters outside Port Hegen harbor. Around noon, one of them, Ralph Hemming, spotted the dolphins.

---

sonar (sō'när), means of interpreting sound waves to detect location of objects and depth of water

"Must be 200, maybe 300 dolphins out there," he said, using the radio that linked the boats and shore. "Haven't seen them this close to shore in years."

Another fisherman's voice came over the radio. "Had some up to the Cape last year. Paper said a dozen died. Got trapped in shallow water, they said."

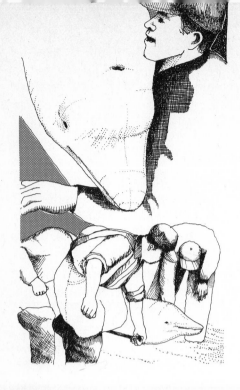

The radio crackled as another voice came in. "Hey, Ralph. You got Spooner with you?"

Hemming swung his rumbling boat towards a bright red float that marked one of his sunken traps. He pressed the microphone button. "He's home mending some of our rickety traps."

"Too bad," said the other man. "That Spooner could tell you what kind they are. Yes, and their size and weight and favorite food!"

Ralph Hemming laughed with the others. He hooked the trap line, running the nylon rope over the winch to pull the heavy wooden trap up from the bottom, a hundred feet below.

Like the other men, he took his son, Spooner, with him whenever he could. Spooner knew the sea pretty well for a 14-year-old. He was always reading about the ocean and its creatures. In some ways he knew more than the men who had spent their lives on the water.

But he wouldn't be a fisherman like his dad or his grandfather. Oh, he'd work with the sea all right. Maybe as a scientist or some such. Ralph Hemming wondered what was ahead for Spooner.

* * *

Dolphins! Hundreds of them! Arching out of the water in silver curves!

Spooner could hardly believe his eyes. He dropped the lobster trap he was mending and ran to the end of the wharf.

The dolphins were in the middle of the channel, moving towards Bald Point. He strained his eyes but the fog made it hard to see the dolphins clearly. He'd never seen real dolphins before—only in books or on TV. If only he could get a closer look!

Spooner scrambled down the steps to the pebbly beach. It was dry now, for the tide had begun to ebb. Pushing the rowboat to the water's edge, he floated it and jumped in. He swung the small outboard motor into the water and yanked on the starter rope. The motor buzzed into life.

The fog was getting thicker and the dolphins had disappeared. But Spooner headed the boat out into the channel, then turned towards Bald Point. He knew the waters of this rocky coast by heart.

Even so, he nearly missed the dolphins in the heavy fog. The narrow entrance to Bald Point Cove was only 50 feet wide, with low cliffs rising on either side. Catching a movement in the cove out of the corner of his eye, Spooner swung his boat toward land. Beaching the craft, he sprinted up the low cliff on the side of Bald Point Cove.

The little cove was like a round soup bowl 300 yards across. At high tide, the water in the cove was 20 feet at its deepest. At low tide, the cove was a stretch of wet mud.

Spooner stood looking down on the cove. "Oh, no!" he cried. Below he saw hundreds of dolphins swimming around. But not smoothly, gracefully. Instead, the dolphins darted this way and that, circling, confused. Spooner remembered a story in the paper last year that told how 20 dolphins had died in shallow water near Cape Cod. Scientists had guessed that the deep-sea animals' sonar had failed for some reason.

Now it seemed, it had happened again. Spooner watched as the fast-ebbing tide ran out of the cove like water out of a cracked bowl. He had to get help — fast.

*   *   *

"Listen, Sonny, those dolphins have been living thousands of years without your help." The storekeeper laughed.

"But—"

"And they'll still be swimming in the sea long after you're gone!" The man chuckled.

Spooner closed his eyes. Mr. Shell was the third person in the village he'd talked to. No one took him seriously. No one wanted to help.

"But they're trapped. They're going to die!" blurted Spooner, opening the door. "And people like you don't even care!" He slammed the door behind him.

"Spooner! What's the matter, lad?"

Spooner turned to see Ned Steele coming up from the docks. The old fisherman was 72, but he still worked his traps every day, as he had for more than 50 years.

"It's dolphins, Mr. Steele. Hundreds of them. They're trapped out in Bald Point Cove. And the tide will be out soon!" Spooner quickly told the old man what he had seen.

"I heard on the radio they were close to shore," said the fisherman. "Fog's so thick, everyone's coming in now. Come on. We'll get some help."

*   *   *

A half-hour later, Spooner, Mr. Steele, and nine other fishermen hurried down into the cove. More were on the way. Mr. Steele had radioed the police for help, too.

There wasn't much time left. The water in the cove was only three feet deep and getting lower every minute.

Already there were a few dolphins stuck in the mud on the edge of the cove. The others swam frantically in the shallow water. In only about an hour, all the water in the cove would be gone.

Making a line, Spooner and the fishermen moved into the water from the land. They herded the dolphins toward the narrow bottle-neck opening to the sea. Spooner cheered as some of the dolphins slipped out through the opening.

More people came. Joining the line, they herded more and more animals out to sea. But many others darted about desperately.

"Spooner," Mr. Steele called. "Row out to my boat and radio for some nets. Hurry!"

Spooner splashed through the shallow water, climbed the cliff, and slid down the other side. He rowed quickly

out to the lobsterman's boat anchored in the channel. In a few minutes, he made contact with Port Hegen, and the nets were on the way. Spooner rushed back to the cove.

When the water had all gone out of the cove over 70 dolphins were left stranded. Using heavy nets, the fishermen tugged and yanked and slid twenty more of the heavy dolphins out into the channel.

At last they could save no more. Spooner stood quietly with his father, Mr. Steele, and the other fishermen.

"That's the best we can do," the old man said.

Spooner's lip trembled. He looked around the cove. All those beautiful animals, stranded alive. They'd be dead by morning.

Ralph Hemming put his hand on his son's shoulder. "You did your best, Spooner. That's all you can ever do."

"Aye," said Mr. Steele. "And if it hadn't been for you, there would be hundreds of dolphins dying here. Think of the ones we saved."

Spooner blinked away tears. "If we knew why they did it, maybe we could have saved all of them."

Spooner's dad smiled to himself. He could see Spooner was off on another search. The way Ralph looked at it, you can't figure out every one of life's mysteries. But Spooner would track it down. He'd find out why those dolphins behaved the way they did.

That was what was special about Spooner. He was determined to find out the answers. And he never gave up. Ralph's smile broadened, and he hugged his son's shoulder. Spooner loved the sea and its creatures as much as his dad or his grandfather did. Whatever was ahead for Spooner, the sea would be a part of it.

94

This is the story of the dolphin disaster as it appeared in the newspaper. Is it as interesting as the fiction story?

Dolphins Stranded in Bald Point Cove
Young Boy Leads Rescue — Saves Over 300

PORT HEGEN, MAINE, Sept. 28 — A local boy's hobby and some quick-thinking helped him save almost 300 white-sided Atlantic dolphins yesterday. More than 50 of the dolphins died when they were stranded by a fast-ebbing tide in Bald Point Cove, about two miles east of this small fishing village.

"The white-sided dolphin lives in deep water," Dr. Eduardo Montez, head of the Sloan Aquarium, said yesterday. "They probably became confused in shallow water and could not find their way out of the cove," the scientist said.

Dr. Montez will lead a team of scientists in a study of the dead animals. "We want to learn more about what caused this disaster," he said.

First Sightings

The dolphins were first spotted shortly after noon on Saturday by lobster fishermen tending their traps near Port Hegen. They watched the dolphins move past the harbor, then around Bald Point on the east end of the harbor.

Then 14-year-old Spofford ("Spooner") Hemming, who lives near Bald Point, saw the dolphins. To get a closer look, he went out in a rowboat with a small outboard motor. He found the dolphins in Bald Point Cove, a narrow-mouthed inlet which is dry at low tide.

"There were hundreds of dolphins in the cove," the boy later said. "It was a great sight, but I knew something was wrong." The boy, whose hobby is studying the sea and its creatures, explained: "Dolphins are terrific swimmers. But those in the cove darted this way and that. Their movements were jerky. The water was getting lower all the time, and they couldn't seem to find the way out of the cove. I had to do something."

Race Against Time

Returning to Port Hegen, Spooner looked for help. "Low tide was at 4:17 Saturday," he said. "That meant I had about two hours to save the dolphins."

In Port Hegen, the boy persuaded a small group of fishermen to return with him to the cove. The men made a line and walked out into the water. They were able to herd some of the dolphins toward the narrow opening leading to the sea. Many of them funneled their way out of the cove, but, as the tide went out, more than 70 dolphins were stranded.

More fishermen were alerted by radio to bring their nets to the cove. With their help, the rescuers managed to drag about 20 dolphins out to deep water. The rest could not be saved.

"It was a terrible disaster for the dolphins," said Dr. Montez. "If it had not been for the Hemming boy, it would have been much worse."

ACTIVITY 1

Fact Questions (Fiction Story)

1. Where did this story take place?

2. How old was Spooner Hemming?

3. What was Spooner's hobby?

4. How did Spooner know the dolphins were in trouble?

5. Who finally agreed to help Spooner?

ACTIVITY 2

Fact Questions (Newspaper Story)

1. Where is Port Hegen?

2. Who is Dr. Montez?

3. What is Spooner's first name?

4. On what day of the week did the disaster happen?

5. What time was low tide that day?

ACTIVITY 3

Thought Questions

Use information from both the fiction story and the newspaper story to help answer these questions.

1. What do you think the lobstermen used their radios for?

2. In what ways did Spooner help his father?

3. Why did Spooner go after the dolphins?

4. Why do you think the storekeeper did not help Spooner?

5. Why do you think the fishermen were willing to work so hard to save the dolphins?

6. What other things might they have done to save the dolphins?

7. What might be a reason for the dolphins' getting lost?

8. Why do you think people like dolphins?

9. Why was Spooner's father proud of him?

10. Do you think the event was a sad one or a happy one for Spooner?

11. Do you think that what Spooner did was worthwhile?

ACTIVITY 4

Understanding Character in a Story

On the left is a column of things people did or said in the fiction story. On the right is a column of characteristics or qualitites belonging to people in the story. Match the action or words on the left with the characteristic or quality in the person that these actions

96

or words best show. *Example:* The answer to 1 could be C or E, but C is better.

1. Ralph Hemming wondered about what Spooner would do for a living.
2. Spooner asked three people for help even though he kept being turned down.
3. Mr. Steele told Spooner to radio for nets.
4. The storekeeper laughed.
5. Spooner recognized that the dolphins were acting strangely.
6. Spooner knew the local waters by heart, even in fog.
7. Spooner's eyes filled with tears.
8. Ralph Hemming said, "You did your best, Spooner."

A. Mr. Steele thinks ahead.
B. The storekeeper probably doesn't take young people seriously.
C. Ralph Hemming is fatherly and wants to set his son on the right path.
D. Spooner is sympathetic to animals in pain.
E. Ralph Hemming is consoling and encouraging.
F. Spooner is well-informed about creatures of the sea.
G. Spooner spends a lot of time in the boat and remembers what he sees.
H. Spooner is persistent.

5
ACTIVITY

**Differences
Between Fiction
and News Stories**

Some of the following pieces of information were in the fiction story, and some were in the news story. Write *Fiction* on your paper and after it the numbers of all those items which were in the fiction story, but *not* in the news story. Write *News* and after it the number of all those items which were in the news story but *not* in the fiction story. Then go on to the next set of questions.

1. Ralph Hemming was sure that Spooner would work with the sea.
2. The dolphins were rescued on September 27.
3. The white-sided dolphin lives in deep water.
4. Spooner felt like crying to think the stranded dolphins would die.
5. Spooner was excited to see the dolphins and dropped his work to follow them.
6. Low tide was at 4:17 Saturday.
7. Ralph Hemming felt proud of his son.

Look back over your answers. You will notice two things:

1. Most of the sentences you selected as part of the fiction story in Activity 4 told about people's private thoughts or feelings.

2. Most of the sentences you selected as part of the news story told facts that more than one person knew and that can be checked with these other sources.

Often in social studies we read about new fields of knowledge. Learning these new things is important for they can affect our lives in unexpected ways. New discoveries can lead to new industries, new towns, changes in people's lives, and growth in many directions.

In the next reading, be alert to the many changes that may come from the new science of oceanography. Look also at the new occupations, one of which might be for you.

Ralph Hemming knew that Spooner loved the sea. And he thought his son might be a scientist some day. Do you think Spooner would like to work in oceanography? Read the article to find out if you yourself might like to be an oceanographer.

Oceanographers at Work

Written by Walter Harter.[2]

"Whale in trouble!"

The report came from a shrimp boat near Florida's east coast. A launch sped away from a sea-research station. It was stocked with special equipment to help ocean creatures. Three young oceanographers were on board.

A little more than two miles offshore, James Hall, who was in the bow as lookout, saw the afternoon sun reflect from a long gray object that appeared to roll across the crest of the waves. He motioned with his arm, and the young man at the wheel throttled down.

What lay lazily in the trough of the waves wasn't just one whale, but two—a mother gray whale and her baby.

Apparently the whales were resting, rising and falling with the movement of the waves, and occasionally shooting spouts of water and vapor into the air from their blowholes. They were in no trouble and would soon move on. But the young oceanographers realized that this was a rare opportunity to record any sounds that might show communication between the two creatures.

oceanographer (ō shə nog′rə fẽr), one who studies the ocean

oceanography (ō shə nog′rə fē), branch of geography dealing with the ocean

sediment (sed′ə mənt), that which settles to the bottom of a liquid

aquanaut (ak′wə nôt), person who lives in an underwater chamber in order to make experiments and learn more about the ocean

The launch rode the waves while James Hall, in swim trunks and life jacket, slipped over the side. In his right hand was a microphone, its wire unraveling from a container strapped to his back.

For more than an hour, young Hall swam close to the whales, the microphone dangling in the water. He could not hear anything, but he knew that water was an excellent transmitter of sound. The microphone would record anything the whales might be "saying" to each other.

That night, the oceanographers played the tapes. They heard crooning sounds, the kind a mother would make to her child. But the language was so different from any they knew, it could have come from another planet.

The tapes were played at normal speed, then replayed very slowly, and again extremely fast. The sounds were compared with the sounds oceanographers had already recorded from captive porpoises and whales. After extensive studies, a pattern of a kind of "speech" has already been confirmed. If some kind of communication can be established between man and sea creature, the results will be worth the years of research.

While James Hall was swimming around the whales in the Atlantic Ocean, other sea scientists were dropping depth charges into the Pacific Ocean. They were trying to prove or disprove a theory. The theory was that

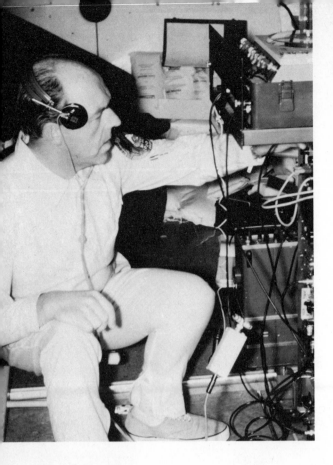

ing in a metal capsule lying on the bottom of the ocean. Just as astronauts spend long periods of time in outer space, so do aquanauts stay for long periods beneath the sea.

Not so long ago, the oceans were thought of only as a highway where ships could sail from place to place. Now, in all parts of the world, men and women are studying the seas and oceans, and the plants and animals that live in them. The entire world is becoming aware of the importance of the oceans as a source of food and minerals. We are realizing that to protect the oceans from pollution is the business of everyone.

So far, oceanographers have found and classified more than 20,000 kinds of fishes. They study the habits of fish in order to help us get more fish from the sea. They are now able to tell fishermen when their fleets should put to sea and where to drop their nets.

According to these scientists, the oceans will soon give up many more things than food. All the minerals found on land are in the sea, and in greater quantities. Oil, iron, copper, and coal will soon be mined beneath the water. It is a fact that the rich sands that led to the gold finds in Alaska extend far out to sea. Even diamonds are being mined from the seas.

For young people who like to solve problems and puzzles, and who are attracted to the sea, oceanography offers many opportunities. It is a science that uses a variety of skills. Computer programmers, divers, photographers, electricians, office personnel, and many others help in ocean research. All of these people are explorers on one of our last frontiers.

the continents were once one big land mass. They may have been split apart by undersea volcanoes and earthquakes.

In another experiment, scientists were measuring the heat given off by the ocean floor. Others were emptying hollow metal tubes that had been driven into the sediment on the ocean floor. When they were brought up, they were filled with living organisms. Some could only be seen with a microscope. Some no human eye had ever seen before. The sediment can also be examined for mineral deposits. The floor of our deepest oceans has never been exposed to air and sunlight. It has remained the same since earth was formed.

In still another part of the world, five women called aquanauts were liv-

ACTIVITY 1

Fact Questions

Like most social studies articles, "Oceanographers at Work" included a number of interesting facts. To see how well you understood them, look back at the article and write the answers to these questions.

1. How could the microphone record sounds that James Hall could not hear?

2. If the continents were once one big land mass, what could have split them apart?

3. Name three pieces of scientific equipment mentioned in this article.

4. Why is it important to protect the oceans from pollution?

5. Why are oceanographers explorers?

ACTIVITY 2

Practically all learning becomes useful sooner or later. Sometimes new discoveries are helpful right away. At other times, the usefulness of a new discovery is not seen for a long time. In Column I are various fields of study that interest oceanographers now. In Column II are some uses that have come or may come from these studies. Match the number of the study with the letter of the closest possible use.

I

1. study of the habits of fish

2. study of languages of porpoises and whales

3. living in an underwater capsule for weeks

4. classifying species of fish and plants

5. studying sediment brought up from the sea bottom

II

A. learning to communicate with sea creatures

B. growing fish and plants useful to man in underwater "farms"

C. giving necessary information to fishing fleets

D. mining mineral deposits

E. construction of permanent living or work places under water

HOW TO READ IN SCIENCE

Have you ever shopped for groceries at a supermarket? As you move through the aisles, what makes the job easier? The foods and other products are arranged in groups. Clothing stores, furniture stores, hardware stores, all arrange things in groups. It would be hard to find a certain book in the library if the books were not arranged in groups. Remember when you visited the zoo? There was a monkey house, a reptile house, a bird house.

There are more than 1½ million different kinds of plants and animals on earth. It would be hard to read and learn about them all if scientists had not divided them into groups. It is much easier to remember them when we know how they are grouped. In this reading, notice how seaweed and sea shells are grouped.

Often when we go to the seashore, we pick up shells and take home a collection. Unlike Spooner, we do not often find out what sort of creature lived in each shell. Would you like to start a shell collection? Read on to find out the things you'll need to know.

Sea Shells

Written for this book
by Leonard Bernstein.

Seashells are the coverings of soft-bodied sea animals. Most shells that people collect are empty. The animals that once owned them belong to the second largest group of animals known, the mollusks. Mollusks are among the oldest groups of living things. Most mollusks live along the shores and in shallow waters. Some live at great depths in the oceans. Others inhabit fresh waters or may even live on land.

Seashells have been used by many people in different ways. Some American Indians used seashells as money. It was called wampum. Mother-of-pearl is the smooth, shiny inside layer of some kinds of shells. It is still used for buttons and jewelry. The shell of the windowpane oyster is usually clear and colorless. It is used to make lampshades and other ornaments.

Seashells are divided into four main groups. Let's examine each of them.

algae (al'jē), a group of simple plants containing chlorophyll

chlorophyll (klôr'ə fil'), the green coloring matter of plants

mollusk (mol'əsk), any of a group of animals with a soft body enclosed in a shell

chiton (kī'tən), a mollusk with a tough protective shell

bivalve (bī'valv), any mollusk having two shells hinged together

Chitons

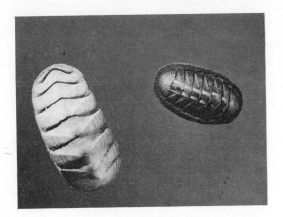

Chitons

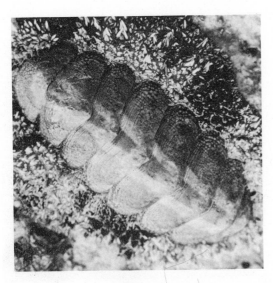

Chiton

Bivalves

Quahog

Scallop

Chitons are the most primitive of all mollusks. The shell is made up of eight plates, arranged one after the other. Each plate rests on the one following. Some chitons are less than one inch (2.5 centimeters) long, but Steller's chiton may grow to 11 inches (28 centimeters).

Bivalves are two-shelled mollusks. Each shell is joined to the other at a hinge. The most common bivalves are the oyster, scallop, mussel, clam, and giant clam. The color and design of scallop shells make them a delight to collectors.

Sea Snails

Tiger Cowry

Turban Shell

Tusk Shells

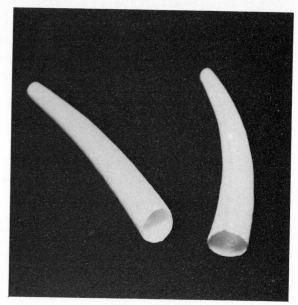

Money Tusk

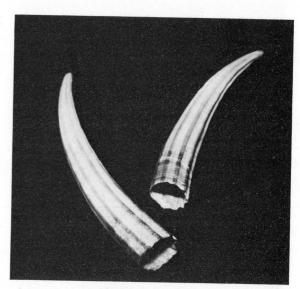

Elephant's Tusk

Sea snails are a very large group of mollusks. Most of these animals have a single spiral shell. Many of the most attractive shells belong to this group. They are the most prized by collectors. Among the more common of these shells are the limpet, top shell, turban shell, cowry, conch, and whelk.

Tusk shells look like little elephant tusks. Sometimes they are called tooth shells. They are hollow tubes that curve and are smaller at one end. Both ends are open. Some shells in this group are ivory tusk, comma tusk, and elephant's tusk.

104

ACTIVITY

1. Do most mollusks live on land or in the sea?

2. Into how many main groups are the seashells divided?

3. What are the names of the four main groups of seashells?

4. Which of the mollusks studied are two-shelled?

5. In what group are the shells most prized by collectors?

6. Which group of mollusks is the most primitive?

7. To what group of mollusks do the limpets belong?

8. To what group of mollusks do the oysters belong?

ACTIVITY

On your paper, write the number of each of the sea shells named in Column I. Decide on the group in Column II to which each shell belongs. Write the letter of the group next to the number of the sea shell.

Column I	Column II
1. oyster	
2. comma tusk	
3. turban shell	A. chitons
4. Stellar's chiton	
5. ivory tusk	B. bivalves
6. scallop	
7. conch	C. sea snails
8. elephant's tusk	
9. mussel	D. tusk shells
10. cowry	
11. clam	
12. limpet	

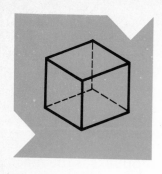

HOW TO READ IN MATHEMATICS

Mathematics has a language of its own. Sometimes we need to translate it into plain English. In this lesson you will read signs and symbols placed together to make mathematical phrases and sentences. When you have learned to read these mathematical phrases and sentences, it will be easy to translate them.

The lobstermen of Port Hegen, Maine, had a ship-to-shore radio on each boat. But if we listened in on a short-wave radio set, we might not understand them. They would be using words about lobstering and seafaring that most of the rest of us don't know. In the same way, sea scientists speaking to each other about their specialty are talking a foreign language, so far as the rest of us can tell. Yet no language is hard for those who speak it.

You know a language besides English. You can already speak a few words of it. Do you want to know what that language is? Read on.

The Language of Mathematics

Written for this book
by William L. Schaaf.

From English to Mathematics

Table I shows some examples of "translating" from English to mathematics. Study the English phrase and the mathematical phrase that follows it. Try to discover the meaning of any mathematical symbol that is new to you. You will find that some ideas may be expressed in more than one way in both mathematics and English.

Table I

English Phrase	Mathematical Phrase
a. A number increased by five	$N + 5$
b. Five more than a number	$N + 5$
c. Three times a number	$3 \times N$; or $3N$; or $3(N)$
d. Half a number	$\frac{1}{2}N$; or $\frac{N}{2}$
e. A number decreased by five	$N - 5$
f. A number diminished by five	$N - 5$
g. Five less than a number	$N - 5$

Answer these questions on your own paper.

1. According to the examples in Table I, what English word did N stand for?
2. According to the table, what English words may this sign + stand for?
3. What English words may this sign − stand for?
4. In example (c) what operation (addition, subtraction, multiplication, or division) is shown by parentheses?
5. In example (d) is N to be multiplied or divided by 2?

From Mathematics to English

The language of mathematics may also be "translated" into English. Study the examples shown in Table II. Notice that a phrase in mathematics may be expressed in more than one way in English.

Table II

Mathematical Phrase	English Phrase
a. $N - 8$	A number decreased by eight; or, a number diminished by eight; or, eight less than a number
b. $2N + 4$	A number doubled and then increased by four; or, a number multiplied by two and then increased by four; or, four more than two times a number
c. $\dfrac{N}{3}$	A number divided by three; or, one-third a number
d. $3(20)$	Three times twenty; or, twenty multiplied by three

Translate each of these English phrases into a mathematical phrase which means the same thing. You may use Tables I and II to help you. Write the answers on your own paper.

1. Five more than twice a number
2. Seven times a number
3. A number divided by fifteen
4. A number diminished by twenty
5. A number increased by twelve
6. Three more than half a number
7. A number doubled and then increased by sixteen
8. A number decreased by forty
9. Five more than three times a number
10. Twenty less than a number

107

Improve Your Reading Rate

The amount of reading that you have to do becomes heavier each year as you pass through school. If you can learn to read more rapidly, it will be very helpful to you.

The first thing to do in increasing your speed is to get rid of any bad reading habits that you may have. The habits listed below will prevent you from reading fast. Check yourself.

Answer these questions with "Yes" or "No." Write on your own paper.

1. Do you move your lips when reading silently?
2. Do you point to words with your finger as you read?
3. Do you move your head from side to side as you read?
4. Do you often retrace a line with your eyes because you can't pronounce a word or understand its meaning?
5. Do you read one word at a time?

If you have any of these habits, practice the helps suggested below. Maybe you can suggest other helps of your own.

Overcoming Bad Habits

Lip moving: Hold your finger over your lips or hold a piece of paper between them.

Finger pointing: Hold your book with both hands, one on each side of the book.

Head moving: Rest your chin in the palm of one hand and hold it still.

Re-tracing lines: Work hard on pronunciation and meaning helps given in this book.

Reading one word at a time: Try to take in several words at each glance.

The Secret of Fast Reading

Fast readers know that the real secret of reading fast is to be able to take in entire groups of words at each glance. As soon as you learn to read for *ideas* instead of reading separate words or small groups of words, you are on the road to speedier reading.

You need also to step up your tempo. You walk faster when you want to cover more ground in a short time. Do the same thing with your reading.

The two most important things to remember in learning to read fast are (1) to read in thought units; and (2) to force your eyes along the lines of print as fast you can make them move.

Here is a paragraph which is marked off into word groups. See if you can read it by taking in each entire group of words in one quick glance.

> Bertela lives / on an island / that belongs / to Denmark. There are / beech trees / in the woods / near her home. Every fall / she gathers beechnuts / in these woods. / The squirrels gather / the nuts, too. / The nuts are so plentiful / that there are / enough of them / for both Bertela / and the squirrels.

Check Your Reading Rate

Below is a selection which can be used to check your reading speed. Your teacher will probably give this test to you. If you should work by yourself, first study the pronunciation and meanings of the words at the bottom of the page. Use a watch or a clock with a second hand. Start on an even minute, such as 5 minutes past 10 o'clock. Write the time you start the story on your paper. Then read the story. As soon as you finish, look at the clock and write the time you ended.

Alone on an Island Written by Murray T. Pringle[3]

Alexander Selkirk was a nice, average boy. There was only one thing unusual about him—he had the most terrible temper! His family, his friends, everyone, warned him that he should learn to control his temper.

He tried counting up to ten whenever he felt his temper rising, but it didn't work. He never seemed able to get past number three before he exploded. Then he said things for which he later was sorry.

But Alex was also stubborn. Even when he knew he was wrong, he just would not apologize. The time was to come when that stubborn temper was going to get him into real trouble.

It happened this way. One day in the year 1695 he and his closest friend, Dampier, decided to seek a little adventure. So they joined the crew of an expedition to the South Seas.

They hadn't been at sea long before Alexander's hot temper got him into trouble—with the captain, no less! Dampier had done his best to keep his hot-tempered friend under control. But this time he was busy elsewhere on the ship.

Alex got into an argument with the captain. The argument grew hotter and hotter. Finally the captain shouted, "One more word out of you, my bucko, and I'll set you down on yonder lonely isle!" He waved angrily at the island which lay to the right of the sailing vessel.

Alex, boiling with anger, retorted, "I'd rather be on a lonely island than continue to sail with the likes of you. By all means, drop me on the island."

"By thunder!" roared the captain. "That's done it!"

Quickly he commanded a few sailors standing nearby, anxiously watching the quarrel. He told them to lower a small boat and take the hot-tempered youth to the island.

The sailors put a few things in a small boat. They included bedding, a hatchet, a knife, a kettle, and some books. They then rowed to the island. Here they left the angry youth and rowed back to the ship.

Alexander Selkirk (al′ig zan′dĕr sel′kŭrk), name of a boy in the story

Dampier (dam′pē ēr), name of a boy in the story who was Alexander's friend

Daniel Defoe (dan′yəl dē fō′), one of the authors who wrote a story about Alexander Selkirk

expedition (eks pə dish′ən), a journey for a special purpose

Alex stood on the beach, glaring at the ship. His anger died down, however, as he watched the vessel disappear slowly from sight. He was alone on an island with no one living on it. He was cut off from the world—perhaps forever!

Hot-tempered and stubborn though he was, Alexander Selkirk was also a brave lad. Instead of crying and feeling sorry for himself, he carried inland the few things given him by the captain. Here he set about making a home for himself.

For four long years Alexander Selkirk lived on that island, striving desperately to stay alive. He had many adventures during those four years, but he managed to live. He was prepared to spend the rest of his life there. But one day he saw something he could not believe—a British ship! It hove to off the island and dropped anchor.

Alex rushed down to the beach and began waving his tattered shirt frantically. A small boat set out from the ship. Soon Alex was on his way to London.

Alex was very happy to be back in England. For a time he was busy renewing his old friendships. The one thing that surprised Alex's old friends was the remarkable change that had come over him. No longer was he the hot-tempered boy they had known four years ago. No matter what was said, Alex never grew angry. His experience with the captain and the lonely island had cured him for all time!

Soon writers began writing stories about Alex's experiences. Several talked with him and wrote books or articles about him. Daniel Defoe finally gathered information from all these sources and wrote a story that still lives on. To make his story more interesting, Defoe added cannibals to the island. He also told how Alex had made a companion out of one cannibal whom he called "Friday." In the true story there were no cannibals on the island.

Defoe also gave Alex another name. In his story he called Alex "Robinson Crusoe."

Now you know how we happened to have this famous story.

Computing Your Rate

To find the total time that it took you to read the selection, subtract your beginning time from your ending time. Then divide the number of words in the selection (695) by your remainder expressed in seconds. If it took you 3 minutes and 5 seconds ($3 \times 60 + 5 = 185$ seconds) to read the selection, you would have read 3.75 words per second ($695 \div 185 = 3.75$). To find the number of words per minute (WPM), multiply your rate per second (3.75) by 60. Your answer would be 225 WPM.

Here is the way this would look on your paper:

	Hr.	Min.	Sec.
Ending time:	10	08	05
Beginning time:	10	05	00
Total time:	-	03	05

$$\frac{\text{No. words}}{\text{No. seconds}} \quad \frac{695}{185} \times 60 = 225 \text{ WPM}$$

ACTIVITY 1 Comprehension Questions

1. What was the one thing unusual about Alexander Selkirk?

2. With whom on the ship did he get into an argument?

3. Did Alex object to going to the island or did he ask to go?

4. Who took Alex to the island?

5. How long did Alex live on the island?

6. How did Alex signal to the British ship to come for him?

7. After Alex returned to England, what change did his friends notice in him?

8. Who wrote a famous story about Alex?

9. What did this writer add to the island in his story?

10. What name did this writer give to Alex?

Give yourself a score of 10 for each correct answer. The total is your comprehension score. It tells how well you understood the story. Record your comprehension score next to your speed (WPM). Your aim is to make the speed go up without letting the comprehension go down. You will have the opportunity for further practice in this book.

More Sounds of Vowels and Their Markings

You know the long and short sounds of *a, e, i, o,* and *u.* You also know the sounds of these vowels when followed by *r.* Now you will be given some markings for vowel sounds followed by *r.* You will also be given some additional sounds of vowels and their markings.

The sounds of vowels when followed by *r* are marked differently in different dictionaries. They are marked below as they appear in the dictionary system used in this book. When you have finished working with this page, check the words below in your dictionary. Find out how they are marked in the dictionary that you use.

More Sounds of *a*

You have had the sound of *a* when that vowel alone appears in a word or syllable and is followed by *r,* as in *far.* Sometimes *a* also has this same sound when it is not followed by *r,* as in *father.* In some dictionaries this sound is marked with two dots above, as: fär.

There is another sound of *a* in words followed by *r.* This sound is found in words in which there is another vowel in addition to *a* in the same syllable, as in *care* and *air.* Say *car.* Now say *care.* Do you notice a difference in the sound of *a* in the two words?

Dictionaries vary greatly in the way they mark the sound of *a* as in *care.* In the marking system used in this book, this sound of *a* is marked in this way: kãr. This is the mark ~.

Say each of the words below. Listen to each one carefully, then mark the *a* in it correctly with one of these two marks: ä or ã. In some parts of the U.S., the *a* in *car* sounds like the *a* in *father,* but the *r* sound almost disappears. Write what you hear in your own part of the country. Use your own paper.

1. care	**3.** fair	**5.** stair
2. bar	**4.** cart	**6.** dare

e and *o* Followed by *r*

You know the sound of *e* followed by *r* as in *her.* The *e* sound when followed by *r* usually has the sound of short *u.* In the marking system used in this book, this sound is marked this way: her—hūr. You also know the sound of *o* followed by *r* as in *for.* This sound is marked this way: for—fôr. In the following list, some words have long *e* and some have long *o.* On your paper, mark these vowels this way: wē, gō. Mark the *e* sound when followed by *r* this way: term—tūrm. Mark the *o* sound when followed by *r* this way: short—shôrt. Look only for the sounds of *e* and *o.* Do not mark any other vowels. Number 1 is done for you.

1. ēqual	**3.** herd	**5.** fern
2. we	**4.** horse	**6.** port

◼ More Sounds of *u*

You know the long and short sounds of *u*. There are two other sounds of *u* that are not used in a large number of words. Still you should know about them.

One of these sounds is the sound of *u* as in *rule*. The other is the sound of *u* as in *full*.

In the marking system used in this book, the sound of *u* as in *rule* is marked in this way: ro͞ol. The sound of *u* as in *full* is marked in this way: fool.

On your paper, write the word and next to it the mark for the sound of *u* that you hear. You will need to listen very carefully as you say these words. These sounds are not so different from one another as are the long and short sounds of o. Example: Number 1 is *true* — o͞o.

1. true	**3.** put	**5.** brute
2. pull	**4.** rude	**6.** bull

◼ *Schwa* Sounds: Marking and Accents

A. In the last unit, you reviewed the *schwa* sound. Here it is again. Remember: the *schwa* sounds like a soft *u*. Answer the questions on your own paper.

1. Pronounce *above*. Did the *a* sound like a soft, short u?

2. Pronounce *given*. Did the *e* sound like a soft, short u?

3. Pronounce *hastily*. Did the *i* sound like a soft, short u?

4. Pronounce *pioneer*. Did the *o* sound like a soft, short u?

5. Pronounce *suppose*. Was the *schwa* in the first or the second syllable?

The *schwa* is a very frequent sound. You will find it in a large number of words in the reading that you do.

Most dictionaries use one sign to represent this sound. This is the sign ə. In the dictionary respelling this sign takes the place of any one of the vowels that has the *schwa* sound. Thus, if you look up *alphabet* you will find it respelled this way: al′fə bet′.

B. Say each of the words below softly to yourself. Write the word divided into syllables on your paper. Place the accent mark where it belongs. There is one *schwa* sound in each word. Underline the letter which gives the *schwa* sound. The first one is done for you.

1. dark′<u>e</u>n	**5.** si lence
2. com mon	**6.** post man
3. ma chine	**7.** par a graph
4. a mount	**8.** sug gest

Now look at all of the words. Does the *schwa* sound which you underlined in each word come in an accented or unaccented syllable?

9. Select the correct word in the parentheses and write it on your paper:

The *schwa* sound falls in an (accented, unaccented) syllable.

113

Refreshing Your Dictionary Skills _____

◼ Increasing Your Skill in Working with the Alphabet

In order to use a dictionary rapidly and easily you must be skilled in working with the alphabet. Of course you know the alphabet, but you may need to increase your speed in using it. See how quickly you can do the activities on this page.

A. On your paper, write these words in alphabetical order, looking at the first letter only. If a word is followed by a comma, a period, or another word, copy those down also. If a word begins with a capital letter, write it that way. You will know you have arranged the words correctly when you read the sentences that result.

fish,	All	Some	waters	boat	captains	eat
peaceful,	incomes, or	don't	get	rivers.	travel	unexciting
journey	miles	over	quiet	long	yearly.	huge

B. If you are to find a word quickly in a dictionary, you need to look at the letters that follow the first letter. A message is hidden below. To find it, choose the word in each pair which comes first in alphabetical order. As you choose each word, write it on your paper.

1. The – things
2. mast – man
3. who – without
4. water – waits
5. four – for
6. his – hits
7. shirt – ship
8. two – to
9. cook – come
10. in – is
11. always – arrives
12. misses – mistakes
13. throwing – the
14. boat – boom

C. Pair off the words in this list according to the first letter. Then look at the second (or third) letter in each word in the pair and decide which of the two comes first. Write them on your paper in alphabetical order. The two words beginning with *f* will be the first pair. *Fifty* comes before *fish* in the alphabet, so the first word in your sentence will be *Fifty*.

swam	fish	waves	thunderous
warm	through	swiftly	fifty

D. Make another sentence by writing these words in alphabetical order on your paper:

mice	Agnes	large	shrieked.	after	prettily,
found	prancing	male	four	she	lazy

Making Use of Guide Words

You probably know that at the top of each page in a dictionary there are two words. These are the "guide words." They tell you whether or not the word you are looking for is on that page. The first guide word tells you what the first word on the page is, and the second guide word tells you what the last word on the page is.

When you are looking up the meaning of a word, always note the alphabetical arrangement within the word you are looking for. Then glance at the guide words. Find the guide words that tell you that the alphabetical arrangement you are looking for is on that page.

Below are some guide words as they might appear at tops of pages in a dictionary. See how quickly and how well you can make use of these guide words by doing the next exercise. Write the answers on your own paper.

magnet	430	mamma
mammal	431	maple
march	432	may

1. What is the first word on page 430?
2. What is the last word on page 431?
3. What is the first word on page 432?

On your paper, write the one word in each group that would appear on the page given. Read the words in order and you will have a sentence.

4. 431   mail   many   matter

5. 432   marvelous   make   maps

6. 430   marble   mark   maids

7. 432   mane   may   major

8. 432   marry   manager   mailmen

9. 431   manly   mattress   mask

10. 430   masters   males   maples

Working with Prefixes and Suffixes

You know that a prefix is one or more syllables placed at the beginning of a word. You also know that a suffix is one or more syllables placed at the end of a word.

Often, when you come to a long word, you will find that it has a prefix or suffix, or perhaps both. If you separate the prefix or suffix from the base word, perhaps you will find that you can pronounce the whole word. Prefixes and suffixes also help you to understand the meanings of words.

Working with Prefixes

Here are some common prefixes and some of their meanings. Review those you have had before. Study carefully the ones that are new to you.

Prefix	Meaning	Example
pre	before	preview
de	do the opposite of	decamp
semi	half, partly	semiannual
super	over, above	superhuman
trans	across, over, through	transport
inter	between, among a group, one with another	interlock
bi	twice, double, two	bicycle
sub	under, below	subway

Prefix Word Game

Your teacher will give you a copy of this crossword puzzle. This is the way to work it: Use one of the prefixes in the list to make a word that fits each sentence. The first phrase tells you what the word means.

Write ACROSS words in the spaces going across and DOWN words in the spaces going down. The number tells the number of the space where you should start writing. For example, Number 1 Across is *transatlantic*.

Across

1. Across the Atlantic. The Millers sailed to France on a _____ liner.
5. Every two weeks. The group held _____ meetings.
7. A view ahead of time. Billy saw a _____ of the movie.
8. Ways or passages under the ground. People in New York City use _____ to get to work.
10. Men with powers above the normal. The planet was inhabited by _____.
11. A plane with two main wings. I've never flown in a _____.
12. Between the states. We drove on an _____ highway.

Down

1. Carry from one place to another. He plans to _____ the goods by truck.
2. Half a circle. The class sat in a _____ around the teacher.
3. Across the world. Joan flew on a _____ airline.
4. Woven between. The threads in the bedspread were carefully _____.
6. Take the frost from. Mrs. Banks had to _____ her refrigerator.
8. The layer of soil beneath the surface layer. When Mr. Robinson was digging, he found that the _____ was hard.
9. Extra fine. Tom liked _____ sugar on his berries.

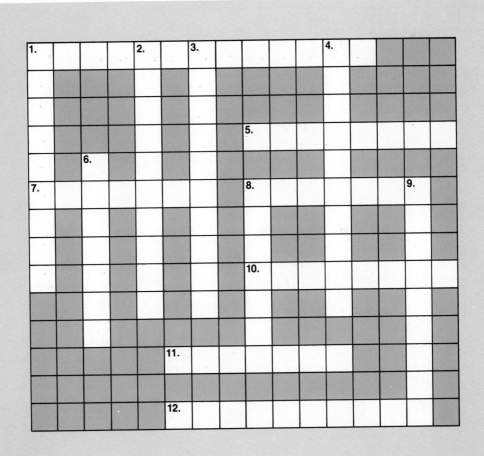

◤ Working with Suffixes

Here are some common suffixes. Review the ones you have had before. Study carefully the ones that are new to you.

Suffix	Meaning	Example
ment	state or condition of	excitement
less	without, that has no, that does not	helpless
able	that can be, suitable to	comfortable
ure	state of being	pressure
an or *ian*	native or inhabitant of	Italian
ship	state or condition of	kinship
ist	a person who does or makes	tourist
ous	having much, full of	joyous
let	little	playlet

◤ Suffix Word Game

Your teacher will give you a copy of this crossword puzzle. Use one of the suffixes in the list to make a word that fits each sentence. The first phrase tells you what the word means. When there are two suffixes with the same meaning, choose the one that gives you a familiar word.

Write ACROSS words in the spaces going across and DOWN words in the spaces going down. The number tells the number of the space where you should start writing.

Across

1. State of being disappointed. It was a great _____ to Tom when he couldn't go to camp.
6. One who does art work. The painting was done by a famous _____.
7. State of being a king. _____ has its problems.
9. Without care. Sue was _____ in her schoolwork.
10. That can be liked. Ann is a very _____ person.
11. State of being pressed. The car stopped because of the _____ of his foot on the brake.

Down

1. Suitable to drink. Ink is not a _____ liquid.
2. That is likely to perish. The box of fruit was marked "_____."
3. Native or inhabitant of Europe. Jane was born and raised in Europe and was proud to be a _____.
4. That does not become tired. Sally is a _____ worker.
5. Full of joy. It was a _____ day.
8. Little isles. The boat wandered among the _____.

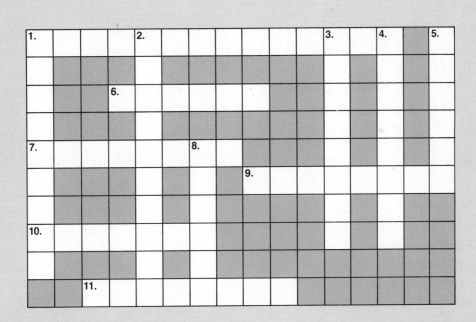

Outlining Paragraphs

You made diagrams of paragraphs in the previous unit. In these diagrams you showed the main idea of each paragraph together with the details related to it.

The main idea and details of a paragraph may also be shown in outline form. You will have practice in outlining paragraphs on this page. Read each paragraph. Then outline it on your paper. The first paragraph has been outlined for you. Use the same form. List the main idea and three details for each paragraph. Number the paragraphs 2 to 6. Label the details A, B, and C.

1. The oyster is a shellfish that produces pearls. This happens when a small particle gets inside the oyster's shell. The animal deposits a pearly substance around this particle. Layer after layer of this substance is deposited. After a rather long period of time, a pearl is formed.

Main idea: The oyster is a shellfish that produces pearls.

Details:
A. This happens when a small particle gets inside the oyster's shell.
B. The animal deposits a pearly substance around this particle.
C. Layer after layer of this substance is deposited.
D. After a rather long period of time, a pearl is formed.

2. The soft-shelled clam has two useful tubes. The clam raises them up above the surface when the tide comes in. One tube draws in oxygen and food particles. The other tube lets out carbon dioxide and waste products.

3. The scallop is a great traveler. It does not form beds or fasten itself to rocks. It keeps moving by clapping its two shells together. In olden times, travelers sometimes wore a scallop shell to show that they had taken long journeys.

4. It is well worth a search to find the beautiful shells of land snails. Many can be found in our Southern states. They are best hunted at night and can easily be found with a flashlight. During the day they can be found under stones and logs.

5. The beautiful turban shells are in great demand. These shells are usually found in the Indian Ocean. They are heavy and are shaped very much like a turban. Shell collectors treasure the green turban, which is the giant of the turban family.

6. The abalone shell is beautiful and useful. Both the inside and outside take a high polish. It provides the pearly, shiny material known as mother-of-pearl. Buttons and various kinds of jewelry are often made from this popular shell.

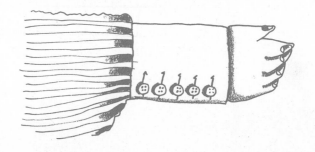

5

A Changing Land

**HOW TO READ
LITERATURE**

The *theme* of a story is its main idea. If you can sum up the whole story in one sentence, that is probably its theme. Often the main thing that happened to the main person tells us the theme. The title of a story often gives you a clue to the theme.

In the next story, the main thing that happened to the main person is *Tensing Norgay conquered Everest.* Notice how all the other elements of the story fit into the theme. The *setting* is Mount Everest, highest mountain in the world. It is also Nepal and India where Tensing spent his life. The *characters* are Tensing and Hillary, both determined and courageous climbers. The *plot* is the series of events that takes them to the top. The *conflict* is their battle against the climate, against fatigue, and against their own wandering minds, as well as against the mountain. Everything in the story tells us more about this effort and achievement.

But a fiction story also tells us how the characters felt and what they thought. So the theme is not complete until we add what this experience meant to the main person. The theme of a story must include more than what happened. It is more than "Tensing conquered Everest." Perhaps it is "How Tensing conquered Everest and what it meant to him." Read to find out what this experience meant to Tensing.

Have you ever run in a race to the point where you wanted to drop—and then you made yourself run some more? Some people like to push themselves to their limits. It is not always wise. Yet, afterwards, there is a feeling of satisfaction.

That is what happened to the Nepalese mountain climber, Tensing, in the next story. Read to find out how it felt to climb Everest for the first time.

The Conquest of Mount Everest

Written for this book
by Glenn Munson.

Tensing woke slowly. What was that? A sound like a high-pitched wail. Was it the gods who live at the very top of Mt. Everest? No one knew what might be on that peak. No one had ever been there. The noise grew louder.

Tensing tried to think. He and his climbing partner, Edmund Hillary, were camped in a small tent at 27,900 feet (8,504 meters)—more than five miles high. What oxygen they could spare for the night was gone. Without it, even a strong mountaineer weakened in this thin, crystal-clear air. A step of six inches could take great effort. The mind slowed down too. It was hard to think, to keep the mind from straying. Many climbers had died at these great heights for that reason.

The roar grew louder now, rushing down on them. Tensing hunched himself inside his sleeping bags, pressing against the mountain.

Then the roar was all around them,

scale (skāl), to climb up or over

Sherpa (shūr′pə), a member of a Tibetan people living in Nepal

and the wind hammered the tent like a giant fist. The tent flapped wildly as the wind tore at it, trying to pluck it from the ropes that held it down.

Others had tried to scale Everest before this. Eleven large expeditions and several smaller ones had attempted to conquer Mt. Everest, for it was the highest peak in the world, 29,028 feet (8,848 meters). An Englishman, Mallory, led the first expedition in 1921. He was driven back by strong winds, bitter cold, and the thin air. When Mallory was asked why anyone would want to climb Everest, he replied, "Because it's there."

In 1922, he led another expedition —and was lost in a swirling blizzard high on the mountain. Others died on the mountain too. No one had ever reached the top.

Tensing Norgay, a Sherpa from the high valleys of eastern Nepal, had come as close to the top as any one. Tensing first climbed Everest in 1935. He was then a 21-year-old porter. After that, he had joined five other Everest expeditions. With much experience on other mountains, he had become one of the world's best mountain climbers.

In 1952, Tensing and another climber scaled the heights of Mt. Everest. But they were low on food, had no sleeping bags, and the winter storms were coming. They had to give up and turn back without reaching the top.

The bitter cold and great strain had weakened Tensing. He needed months of rest to regain his health. But when he heard that the British were planning an expedition he wanted to take part. He offered his help, if only to carry supplies to camps part way up the mountain. When the expedition gathered in Nepal in March, 1953, Tensing felt strong enough to join them. It would be his seventh try at scaling the world's highest peak.

By the end of May, the climbers had tested equipment and trained in high altitudes. They had pushed a string of camps up the steep slopes and past the sheer drops of Everest.

On May 28, Tensing and Hillary battled their way to 27,900 feet, where they would make their final camp. A three-man back-up party dropped supplies and turned back to make their weary way to a lower camp. Tensing and Hillary were alone. The final try for the top was up to them.

Working without oxygen—for their supply was dangerously low—they used ice axes to scrape away the snow from a rock slope. It took two hours to chip away the ice-welded stones to clear a space wide enough to pitch their tents. At sundown, they crawled inside, put on all their warm clothing, and wriggled into their sleeping bags— two for each man.

They made a meal of canned soup, fish, fruit, jam, and biscuits. Hillary brought out a special treat, a can of apricots. They were frozen, but soon thawed in the flame of their tiny cooker. This was their dessert. Then Tensing and Hillary settled down to sleep.

The temperature dropped to 27 degrees below zero (−32.8°C.). They had allowed a small supply of oxygen for the night, but it was soon used up. Without the oxygen, it was hard to sleep. Besides, every now and then a sudden powerful wind screamed down the mountain and slammed against their tent.

They were up at four, but it took two and one-half hours to make some breakfast and get ready for their final push. Yet surely the gods of Everest were smiling on them, thought Tensing. The wind had died to an easy breeze, the sun was shining, and the sky was clear.

By nine o'clock Tensing and Hillary stood on the South Peak. Before them was the final ridge to the top. It rose steeply with deep snow hanging over the knife-edge ridge along one side.

Slowly, painfully, the two men moved along on the snow, step by careful step. An hour later, tired and breathing hard, they came to firmer ground— a mass of jagged rocks, the hardest kind of climbing. Worse still, they came up against a rock forty feet high, blocking their way.

The slab of stone rose above them like a wall. Next to it was a great mound of snow which hung over the edge of the mountain. Between this snow mound and the rock was a thin crack just wide enough for one person to squeeze through.

Hillary forced himself into the crack. He pushed himself slowly upward. At any moment, the snow might give away, toppling him off the mountain. Slowly, very slowly, he inched his way up, digging his boot spikes into the icy wall and searching for hand-holds on the sheer rock face. His stomach was tight with fear and he was gasping for breath.

At last he reached the top. He crawled out of the crack onto the rocky ridge. He lay panting for several minutes before tugging the rope to signal Tensing to follow him.

Soon Tensing was up. After a rest, they set out along the ridge, slowly cutting steps in the ice. They hoped each new mound would be the last, but the ridge led up and up, winding its way, it seemed, into space.

They plodded on, inching their way toward the top. Suddenly, Tensing realized that the ridge ahead no longer rose. It sloped down! This must be it—the very top of Mt. Everest, the very top of the world!

Tensing and Hillary stood motionless for a moment. It was hard for them to believe that they had reached the top. Tensing had worked half his life for this moment.

He broke into a grin, and the two men slapped each other on the back. They had made it!

Then, while Hillary took pictures of the view from the top of the world, Tensing knelt down and dug a hole in the snow and ice.

From inside his clothing, he produced some special treats—a chocolate bar, some hard candy, and some biscuits. These he carefully placed in the hole—as his gift of thanksgiving to the gods of Everest, the gods who had allowed him to reach the top of their mountain.

ACTIVITY **1**

Fact Questions

1. Where was Tensing's home?

2. Who was Tensing's climbing partner in this story?

3. How high is Mt. Everest?

4. Who led the first expedition to climb Everest?

5. How old was Tensing when he first climbed Everest?

6. Why did the 1952 expedition fail?

7. What month of the year was it when Tensing and Hillary set out to climb Everest?

8. What did they need to carry with them besides food?

9. What did Hillary do at the top?

10. What did Tensing do at the top?

Above—**Sir Edmund Hillary**; below—**Mount Everest.**

2

ACTIVITY

Thought Questions

1. Why do you think no one had climbed Everest before this?

2. Why do you think Tensing wanted to join the new expedition?

3. Why did the climbers form a string of camps up the mountain?

4. Why did only two make the final attempt?

5. Why did Tensing bury chocolate and candy on top?

6. Why did Hillary take pictures?

7. What other gift to a god or gods do you know about from personal experience?

8. If you could land in a helicopter on top of Everest, would it be the same as what Hillary and Tensing did? Why or why not?

9. How is using a helicopter different from using oxygen tanks?

3

ACTIVITY

In Column I are listed each of the elements of a story. In Column II are those elements in this particular story. Match the name of the element on the left with its description in this particular story on the right.

I	II
1. main characters	A. the struggle of two persons against fatigue, cold, lack of oxygen, and fear
2. setting	B. events one after another of the expedition
3. plot	C. Tensing conquers Everest and also his own fear and physical limitations
4. conflict	D. Mt. Everest, Nepal, and India
5. theme	E. Tensing and Hillary

HOW TO READ IN SOCIAL STUDIES

When you read social studies material you often need to be able to find causes and effects. In social studies you read about events that have happened or conditions that exist. As you read, look for the *cause* of these events or conditions. Ask yourself, "Why did this event happen?" or "Why does this condition exist?"

Events and conditions also have certain *effects* or *results*. As you read, ask yourself, "What effect did this condition have?" or "What was the result of this event?"

If you know how to find causes and effects, you will have a useful aid to reading in social studies.

You are going to read about problems in India. What causes these problems? Often there is more than one cause. The paragraph which describes the problem also tells us the causes. One sentence will sum up the paragraph. It gives you the cause and the result.

The summing-up sentence is much like a main idea sentence. There are word clues to help you identify the summing-up sentence. Look for words and phrases like *because, as a result, caused, resulted in, thus,* and *therefore.*

In the next selection, read each paragraph through once in order to understand the entire situation. As you read, look especially for the summing-up sentence in each paragraph. When you think you have found it, you may have to read the paragraph again to make sure. Remember: you will read about an effect first, and then read about its cause.

The icy peak of Mt. Everest lies between Nepal and Tibet, which is now part of China. The kingdom of Nepal, Tensing's home, was for centuries cut off from the rest of the world by jagged mountains. Nevertheless, Nepal shares much with its southern neighbor, India. Buddha was said to have been born in Nepal. The religion he founded spread through neighboring India to the Orient. Now it interests many people in this country.

Nepal's closeness to India means that it shares much of the same culture. It also shares some of India's many problems.

Why Does India Have So Many Problems?

Written for this book by Marius Livingston.

1. Most of India's people are poor. Their houses are one-room huts made of mud bricks. There is no plumbing in these houses. The people cannot afford electric lights, refrigerators, or telephones. The ordinary villagers have only a few pots to use for cooking and sleep on cots of woven strings. Perhaps they may have one old chair which is kept for a special occasion. They get drinking water from a village well and the water is not always clean and pure. Thus we see that the majority of people in India live under miserable conditions.

2. The farmers of India do not pro-duce enough food to meet the needs of the people. About three-fourths of the people work on very small farms. They do not have modern farm machinery. They do not know about modern methods of farming. As a result, most of the people have little to eat; and if there is a crop failure, many die of starvation.

3. People in India do not have the money to develop their resources. This country has rich deposits of iron ore, coal, and limestone. It also has a large supply of manganese. Chromite and copper are available. Bauxite, from which aluminum is obtained, and salt can be mined in India. But little of India's mineral wealth is used because of lack of funds.

4. It takes years for people to change their attitudes and thinking about a custom such as the caste system. According to this system, the people of Hindu India are divided into different

---

manganese (maŋ'gə nēs), a grayish-white metallic element

bauxite (bôk'sīt), ore from which aluminum comes

Hindu (hin'doo), of the language, culture, or religion characteristic of India

Pakistan (pä'ki stän'), nation west of India

caste (kast), distinct social class determined by birth

129

groups, or castes. Each caste has a definite place in the community. The upper castes have many privileges. The lower castes have few or none. A young person's future depends upon the social level, or caste, of his parents. The caste system was made unlawful a few years ago. The government decided that it would be better for everyone if all people could develop their talents as they wished. Nevertheless, the caste system continues and probably will go on for many more years. Thus, old ways of thinking hold people back from developing themselves fully.

5. In addition to facing problems within its own borders, India feels threatened by Pakistan and China. Both India and Pakistan claim the state of Kashmir. China seems to want to push over its borders and take part of India, as it took Tibet. War always seems close because of these two threatening neighbors.

ACTIVITY 1

Matching Causes and Effects

The effect of each cause in the paragraphs that you just read is printed on the right side of this page. The causes are on the left. On your paper, match the number of the cause with the letter of its effect.

Cause	*Effect*
1. The farmers of India do not produce enough food to meet the needs of the people.	A. Thus we see that the majority of people in India live under miserable conditions.
2. It takes years for people to change their thinking about a custom such as the caste system.	B. As a result most of the people have little to eat; and if there is a crop failure, many die of starvation.
3. India feels threatened by Pakistan and China.	C. People are held back from developing themselves fully.
4. People in India do not have the money to develop their resources.	D. Little of India's mineral wealth is used.
5. Most of India's people are poor.	E. War always seems to be close to the people of India.

ACTIVITY 2

Thinking for Yourself

Write your answers on your own paper.

1. Millions of people in India cannot read. What do you think is the cause of this lack of education?

2. What do you think are the results?

3. What modern inventions might help more people in India to learn to read?

Often you will find accounts in your science books of how scientists have solved problems. This article tells about a few scientists who have tried to solve problems about germs and disease. When they find the *cause* of a disease, they can then more easily prevent or cure it.

In reading this article, or other science material of this kind, first read the entire selection. Gather general information in this first reading. Then go back over the article and look for these things in regard to each person:

1. The full name of the scientist
2. The problem
3. How the problem was solved
4. What was discovered

If more than one problem of a scientist is described, think about each problem and each discovery separately.

Oxygen tanks and masks helped Tensing and Hillary climb Everest. With this modern invention, they could do what no previous generation was able to do. Scientific discoveries may help India solve some of its problems. Modern science helps people all over the world to grow more food and live longer and healthier lives. This is the result of the hard work of many scientists.

What are some of the discoveries of modern science? Who were the discoverers? Read on to find out.

Solving Problems About Bacteria

Anton van Leeuwenhoek

Anton van Leeuwenhoek was a merchant in a little Dutch town. However, he spent much of his time studying science and experimenting.

Leeuwenhoek (lā'vən hook), a Dutch merchant who was interested in science

Pasteur (pas tūr'), a French scientist

Koch (kōk), a German doctor

Lister (lis'tẽr), an English doctor

anthrax (an'thraks), a disease of cattle and sheep, etc., which can be transmitted to humans

Leeuwenhoek's problem was to find a way of magnifying things that were too small to be seen with the human eye. He experimented with lenses and ground hundreds of them by hand. This was very difficult work. Leeuwenhoek was finally able to make fine lenses that could magnify up to 300 times. He used these lenses in making some of the first microscopes.

Leeuwenhoek studied everything he could under these microscopes. He saw

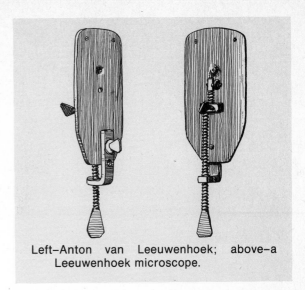

Left—Anton van Leeuwenhoek; above—a Leeuwenhoek microscope.

things never before seen by man. He wrote reports and made drawings of what he saw. These reports proved that he was the first to see bacteria, which are among the smallest living things. Leeuwenhoek is known as the discoverer of the world of bacteria.

Louis Pasteur

Louis Pasteur was a French scientist. One of his first problems was to find out what caused wine to spoil. Using a microscope, he examined wine which had spoiled. He found some small living cells called bacteria. It was the bacteria which caused the wine to spoil. Pasteur called this harmful change in the wine a "disease" of the wine.

He then reasoned, "If bacteria can cause disease in wine, might bacteria also cause disease in animals?" His next problem was to prove that bacteria could cause disease in animals.

His chance came when people in the silk industry in France asked him for help. This industry was near ruin because of a disease that was killing the silkworms. Pasteur conducted careful research to find out what was causing disease in the silkworms. He discovered that there were, in fact, two diseases. Both of these were caused by bacteria. These bacteria grew on the mulberry leaves which the silkworms ate for food. Pasteur showed the silkworm breeders how to prevent the bacteria from forming on the mulberry leaves. Thus he saved the silk industry in France and in other countries.

These are only two examples of Pasteur's research. He made many other important discoveries.

Robert Koch

While Pasteur was conducting his experiments in France, Robert Koch, a German doctor, was also making discoveries about bacteria.

Koch's first problem was to find a way of separating one kind of bacteria from another. This was necessary in order to find out if one type of bacteria caused a certain disease. Koch developed a jelly-like broth in which to raise or grow bacteria. This broth was boiled to kill all bacteria in it. It was then poured into sterilized dishes which

133

Louis Pasteur

Robert Koch

Joseph Lister

were covered to keep out the bacteria in the air. Koch placed only one type of bacteria in this broth. In this way, it was possible to grow a pure colony of one kind of bacteria.

Koch's next problem was to find out if a specific bacteria caused a specific disease. He had seen large numbers of rod-shaped bacteria in the blood of animals that had a disease called anthrax. He grew these bacteria in his sterilized broth. He then injected bacteria from the broth into mice.

The mice developed anthrax. The blood of the mice contained large numbers of the same rod-shaped bacteria he had grown in the broth. Koch had now proved that this specific bacteria caused the disease of anthrax.

Following Koch's experiments, many other scientists studied bacteria and disease. They found that many serious diseases are caused by bacteria. Research of this kind is still going on.

Joseph Lister

Joseph Lister was an English doctor whose discoveries helped make surgery safe. He was a professor of surgery at Glasgow University in Scotland.

At that time, many patients died, not from the surgery, but from infections which followed. Surgery was then a very new procedure. A short time before, surgeons had found that ether could be used as an anesthetic. With the use of ether, they could put a patient into a deep sleep. Surgeons could then perform longer, more complicated operations. Many more people could be operated on and restored to health.

The infections which often followed surgery, however, were a serious problem. Dr. Lister tried to solve it. He knew of Pasteur's work with bacteria. He thought that bacteria in the air might be responsible for infection. If bacteria could be kept from a wound, he reasoned, infection might be prevented.

Lister thought that he might find a chemical that would destroy bacteria. He tried carbolic acid. He found that if this acid was applied to a wound it prevented infection.

But carbolic acid is a very strong chemical. If it is used full strength, it will destroy living tissues. Because of this it could not be used in surgery. Lister would have to find a way of weakening the acid. It took him many years of experimenting, but he finally found that he could do it.

In addition to using carbolic acid to kill bacteria, Lister also made sure that surgeons wore sterilized gloves and used sterilized instruments. He made sure that the operating room was spotless.

At first many doctors scoffed at the things that Lister was doing. However, patients who had undergone surgery in hospitals which used his methods did not develop infections. The death rate was greatly reduced.

Soon surgeons everywhere were using Lister's methods to prevent infection.

1 ACTIVITY

The questions below will show how well you can understand problems, experiments, and discoveries that you read about in science books. When you are asked to name the scientist, write the full name on your paper. Referring to the article, answer the other questions in complete sentences.

1. What was the name of the **first problem solver** mentioned in the article?

2. What problem did he want to solve?

3. What did he do in trying to solve this problem?

4. What did he discover?

5. What was the name of the **second problem solver?**

6. What was the first problem that he undertook?

7. What did he do in solving this problem?

8. What did he find?

9. What was the second problem that he studied?

10. What did he do in solving this problem?

11. What did he find?

12. What was the name of the **third problem solver?**

13. What was the first problem he tried to solve?

14. What did he do?

15. What was the result?

16. What was his next problem?

17. What did he do in solving this problem?

18. What did he prove?

19. What was the name of the **fourth problem solver?**

20. What problem did he try to solve?

21. What steps did he take to solve it?

22. What was the result?

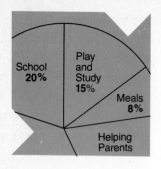

HOW TO READ IN MATHEMATICS

You will find graphs in your social studies, science, and mathematics books. If you can read graphs easily, it will help you to understand the material in these subjects.

To get the facts that you need you must know how to *read* graphs. Special skills are needed in reading graphs in ways that will enable you to get the most out of them. You will have practice in reading graphs in this lesson. You will read about two types of graphs. These graphs will help you "picture" and compare numbers.

Hillary took pictures from the top of Everest. This was one way to prove his accomplishment to the world. It was also a way to share the experience with other people. Pictures give us a kind of understanding that words alone lack.

There are ways to make special kinds of pictures of some of India's problems. These pictures are graphs and charts. They also add to our understanding. Sometimes it takes close attention to interpret these pictures. Read on to find out how.

Reading Graphs

Written for this book
by William L. Schaaf.

Divided Bar Graphs

One type of graph is the divided bar graph. Figure 1 shows a divided bar graph. As you can see, this graph looks like a long bar divided into several parts. A divided bar graph is used to compare different parts of a whole. In this type of graph, the entire bar stands for "the whole." The different sections of the bar stand for parts of the whole.

When you read a divided bar graph, or any other type of graph, be sure to read the title of the graph. The title tells you what the graph is about or what is being compared. Look at the numbers above and below the graph. Then, on your own paper, write the answers to the questions which follow.

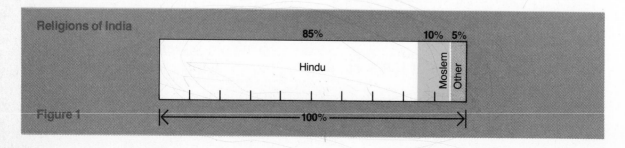

Religions of India — Hindu 85%, Moslem 10%, Other 5% — 100%

Figure 1

136

ACTIVITY 1

1. What is this graph about?

2. What does the numeral under the graph stand for?

3. What do the numerals over the graph stand for?

4. To which religion do most of the people of India belong?

5. To which religion does the next largest group in India belong?

Select the words in the parentheses that best complete the sentence.

6. The graph can be read to find (numbers of people in India, percent of the people who are Christian, names of two major religions in India).

7. The part standing for *Moslem* is (about twice as large; about three times as large; about four times as large) as the part standing for *Other*.

Circle Graphs

Instead of using a bar to represent the whole, or 100%, we sometimes let the whole be represented by a circle. The various parts of the whole can then be shown as appropriate sectors of the circle. A sector of a circle is like a wedge of pie.

When you read a circle graph, be sure to read the title and the explanation of the graph. Figure 2 shows a circle graph. Notice that each part of this circle stands for a percent of the whole. Two parts stand for 20% each, another for 37%, and so on. Below Figure 2 there are some questions which will help you to read this type of graph. Write your answers on your own paper.

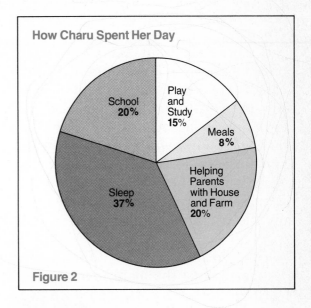

How Charu Spent Her Day

- Play and Study 15%
- Meals 8%
- School 20%
- Helping Parents with House and Farm 20%
- Sleep 37%

Figure 2

ACTIVITY 2

1. What does Figure 2 show?

2. What percent is represented by the entire circle?

3. What is the name of the sector which shows the greatest amount of time?

4. What percentage of the day did Charu spend at meals?

5. Does Charu spend more time at school or more time playing and studying?

137

Finding Minor Details

You have had much practice in finding the main idea. You also have had practice in finding details. Sometimes there are minor details that tell about a major detail. The way to tell the difference between minor and major details is to imagine minor details clustering around a major detail, rather than around the main idea.

Dora the Dinosaur

Dora the Dinosaur had a bath. Her bones had been in a museum for many years. No one had touched them. They had gotten dusty and dirty. One day the curator of the museum said they should be cleaned. Four washers came to give Dora her bath. First they dusted Dora's brittle bones. Then they washed them with rags and water. Finally they covered the bones with a thin layer of varnish.

You probably had no difficulty in discovering that the main idea is *Dora the Dinosaur had a bath.* There are two major details, each with its own group of minor details.

The first explains how Dora became so dusty: Her bones had been in a museum for many years. The second tells more about the bath: Four washers came to give Dora her bath.

Next find the cluster of minor details that are related to the major detail about her dusty bones.

No doubt you found that the details which tell more about her dusty bones are (1) No one had touched them, (2) They had gotten dusty and dirty, (3) One day the curator of the museum said they should be cleaned.

The minor details telling more about the washers are (1) First they dusted Dora's brittle bones, (2) Then

Dora the Dinosaur had a bath.					
Her bones had been in a museum for many years.			Four washers came to give Dora her bath.		
No one had touched them.	They had gotten dusty and dirty.	One day the curator of the museum said they should be cleaned.	First they dusted Dora's brittle bones.	Then they washed them with rags and water.	Finally they covered the bones with a thin layer of varnish.

they washed them with rags and water, (3) Finally they covered the bones with a thin layer of varnish.

Perhaps the block diagram below will help you to get a "picture" of the paragraph.

Some additional paragraphs follow. You are to make block diagrams of these paragraphs on your own paper. Below the paragraphs you will see a block diagram of the first paragraph, which has been partly filled in for you. Copy this diagram on your own paper and finish filling it in. Then use this block diagram as a guide, and make your own block diagrams of the other paragraphs.

1. Scientists can tell how large the dinosaurs were and what they ate. They have two ways of telling the size of dinosaurs. Scientists can put the bones of a dinosaur together to make a skeleton. They can measure footprints left in mud that later hardened into stone. Scientists can tell what dinosaurs ate by the kind of teeth they had. Some ate hard plants. Some ate soft plants. Some ate other animals.

2. Dinosaurs became larger as time went by. The first dinosaurs were small. Many were no larger than a turkey. Their bodies were not heavy, so they walked on their two hind legs. After many, many generations some plant-eating dinosaurs grew large. Some were 80 feet long and weighed 38 tons. They walked on four legs, which helped them to carry their huge bodies. Much of their time was spent in water, which helped support their weight.

3. One dinosaur was particularly dangerous because of its horns and its size. This dinosaur had three horns. One horn was just above its nose. The other two horns were above its eyes. This dinosaur was also very large. It had a gigantic head. The muscles in its neck were thick and strong. The monstrous body and feet of this dinosaur looked very much like those of a rhinoceros.

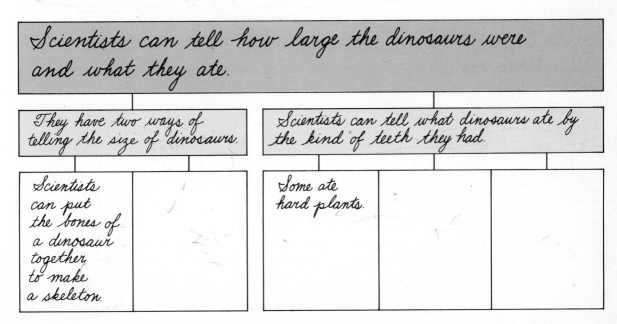

Using an Index in Textbooks _____

Most textbooks have an index. If you are looking for information in a textbook, you will save yourself a lot of time by using the index. You also will be able to find much more information through the use of the index. Usually not *all* information about a topic is given in any one chapter. Bits of information about a certain topic may be found scattered throughout the book. Only the index will tell you where.

Suppose that you had become interested in bacteria while reading the article on "Solving Problems about Bacteria." Suppose you then decided to look for more information about bacteria in a science textbook. You would find an index that looked much like this one.

Do the next exercises to speed up your ability to find facts in a textbook.

A. Using the index on page 140, find the correct page number for each blank below. Write the number of the line on your paper and write the page number next to it.

1. Do you want to know about bats? Page _____ is a good place to be.
2. How does sun affect climate? Turn to page _____ to see.
3. To find out how to plant bulbs, page _____ is a good place to look.
4. If you want to know about birds' eggs, turn to page _____ in the book.
5. Birds can be harmful to man. Turn to page _____ to see why.
6. Look on page _____ if you want to know how birds fly.
7. Are you interested in balloons? Page _____ is the place to turn.
8. What are the types of blood? Page _____ is the place to learn.
9. You'll find out about black widow spiders if you turn to page _____.
10. Find out about beetles on page _____, and now this game is done!

B. Select the best word to fill in each blank from the suggested words that follow. Write the number of the line and the answer on your paper.

Finding topics in an index is really quite a snap.

1. If you were looking up _____, you know you'd find it before *map*.

    farming   regions   tourist

Once you know the secret, it's very simple to do.

2. Present would come after past, and *old* would come _____ *new*.

    before   after

Just look at the topics, and you'll see how to do it.

3. *Climate* would come after _____. That's all that there is to it!

    buildings   geography   explorers

4. It's very clear to see that _____ would come before *border*.

    boxing   bowling   boating

5. Because the topics are arranged in _____.

    order of importance   alphabetical order   their order in the book

Using an Encyclopedia

Among your reference books, encyclopedias are the most exciting. In an encyclopedia you may find information about every topic that interests you.

In a dictionary the words are arranged alphabetically, all in one volume. In an encyclopedia more than one volume is needed to contain all the information. Only topics listed under one or two letters of the alphabet can be placed in one volume. As you know, a letter or a group of letters representing the range of topics in each volume is placed on the spine of the volume. Each volume is numbered.

Have you learned the short cuts in using an encyclopedia? Can you find what you want *very* quickly?

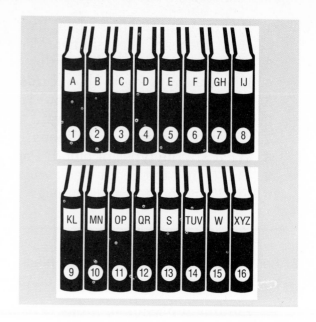

A. Using the picture of the encyclopedia, write the correct number for each space below.

1. You'd do well to look in Volume ＿＿ to learn all about *energy*.
2. And if you care about *reptiles*, Volume ＿＿ is the place to be.
3. You might look in Volume ＿＿ if you're planning a trip to *Spain*.
4. Volume ＿＿ is a good place to try if you want to learn about *rain*.
5. For *India, ink,* and *igloo,* Volume ＿＿ will suffice.
6. Volume ＿＿ is a good place to start if you want to know about *rice*.
7. Volume ＿＿ would be the place to learn about *starfish* or *snow*.
8. But if *aluminum* is your thing, Volume ＿＿ is the place to go.

B. What if your topic is two words? Choose the most important word. People are found usually under the last name. Places are in strict alphabetical order. Write the volume number after the line number on your paper.

1. There's a lot to learn about *Rhode Island*. Volume ＿＿ is the place to look.
2. Do you want to know about *Kind Edward VI?* Volume ＿＿ is your book.
3. To find out all about *Louis Pasteur,* try looking in Volume ＿＿.
4. If you are interested in *Greek art,* you might look in Volume ＿＿.
5. To learn a lot about *Queen Elizabeth II,* Volume ＿＿ is your best bet.
6. If you want to know about *Fort Worth,* ＿＿ is the volume to get.
7. Look up *West Virginia* in Volume ＿＿, and for your next task,
8. Try Volume ＿＿ for everything you always wanted to know about *goblins* and *ghosts* but were afraid to ask.
9. Find *Great Britain* in Volume ＿＿, and when you think of it,
   Encyclopedias can be kind of fun and teach you quite a bit!

Choosing the Right Meaning of a Word _____

Some words have several different meanings. When you look up a word in the dictionary, you often find that two or more meanings are given for the same word. In such a case you need to choose one of these meanings.

How can you tell which meaning to choose? You have to think about the meaning of the sentence in which you find the word. Often it is helpful to think of the meaning of other sentences which surround the one in which the particular word appears. Keep the meaning of these sentences in mind when looking up the particular word. This will tell you which of the meanings best fits into the sentence in which you found the word. You will now have some practice in doing this.

Below you will find dictionary definitions for words which have more than one meaning. The different definitions are numbered 1, 2, 3, and so on. Under these definitions you will find a story using the words in different ways.

Read the dictionary definitions first. Then read the story. Go back to the dictionary definitions to find the right meaning of the word in the sentence. On your paper, write the letters that come before the underlined words in the story. Next to each letter, write the number of the correct definition of the underlined word. For example, the answer to (a) is 2.

FORK **1.** a tool with a handle at one end and points at the other, used to pick up something. **2.** a dividing of something into two or more branches.

RIGHT **1.** just and good, agreeing with law and one's beliefs. **2.** correct or true, agreeing with the facts. **3.** opposite of left.

HARD **1.** firm to the touch, not soft. **2.** not easy to do. **3.** unfeeling, not kind. **4.** causing pain or discomfort, difficult to endure.

WELL **1.** in good health. **2.** a hole dug in the earth to get water, oil, or gas. **3.** in a satisfactory manner.

My name is Amla. I live in a little town in India near the (a) <u>fork</u> of a big river. Some would say I have a (b) <u>hard</u> life.

There is no running water in our house, so my first job is to carry water in a jug from a (c) <u>well</u>. That is a (d) <u>hard</u> job, for the well is at the bottom of a steep hill.

My little brother is sick, and it is my job to take care of him. When he is (e) <u>well</u> again, I can take him outside to play, but now I must stay at home with him. I am teaching him to count. If he gives the (f) <u>right</u> answer, I let him have a piece of (g) <u>hard</u> bread.

After I help to fix dinner, we all sit down for our meal of vegetables and rice. We never eat meat, for in India we do not think it is (h) <u>right</u> to kill any living creature. We eat with our fingers, for we have no (i) <u>forks</u>. The left hand is considered unclean in India, so we eat only with the (j) <u>right</u> hand.

After I have washed the plates, I get ready for bed. I feel proud when my mother says, "Amla, you have done your work (k) <u>well</u>."

Different Ways of Spelling the Same Sounds ____

A vowel may have the same sound even when it is combined with different letters. This sometimes causes trouble, both in spelling and in pronouncing some words. You will now have a chance to work with some vowel sounds that are the same when combined with different letters.

A. *au, aw,* and *al*

Say *cause*. Listen to the sound of *au*. Say *crawl*. Listen to the sound of *aw*. Say *salt*. Listen to the sound of *al*. The *au, aw,* and *al* have the same sound in these words.

Read the first word in each of these lists. Find all other words in each list which have the same vowel sound as the first word. Write these words on your paper.

1. *hawk*, cause, paw, could, raw.   **2.** *ball*, caw, caught, haul, cloud.
3. *fault*, wall, calf, lawn, taught.

◼ Bhondu's Lucky Day (Part I)

Here is a story with some underlined words. In some of them, *au, aw,* or *al* sounds like the *aw* in *paw*. In others, the *a* has a different sound. On your paper, write only those words in which the *a* sounds like the *a* in *paw*. You will find 15 of these words.

My <u>name</u> is Bhondu. I live in a <u>small</u> village in India. The luckiest day of my life was that <u>autumn</u> <u>day</u> I <u>started</u> to school.

I was <u>up</u> at <u>dawn</u> that <u>fall</u> day. I hurried to help my mother <u>haul</u> water from the well and get breakfast ready, <u>because</u> I could hardly <u>wait</u> to get to school. I have <u>always</u> wanted to go to school, but my <u>father</u> never let me go before. It is not his <u>fault</u>, for he needed me to help on the <u>farm</u>. This year he said he could <u>spare</u> me.

I did not have to <u>walk</u> far to get to school. We have no school building in our town. The students sit outside on <u>straw</u> <u>mats</u> on the ground. We have no <u>paper</u> or pencils, for they are too expensive. Instead, we write and <u>draw</u> on <u>slates</u> with pieces of <u>chalk</u>.

That first day at school, I learned to <u>scrawl</u> my name. That <u>may</u> not seem like much, but it is a big thing in a town where <u>almost</u> no one can read or write at <u>all</u>.

B. *ou* and *ow*

Say *out*. Listen to the sound of *ou*. Say *cow*. Listen to the sound of *ow*. The *ou* in *out* and the *ow* in *cow* sound the same.

Find the words in each list in which either *ou* or *ow* has the same sound as *ou* in *out* or *ow* in *cow*. Write these words on your paper.

1. round	sound	howl	though
2. show	fowl	crow	shout
3. count	slow	mouse	down

Bhondu's Lucky Day (Part II)

Here is more of Bhondu's story. Look at the underlined words. There are 15 words in which *ou* or *ow* sound like the *ou* in *out.* When you find the words, write them on your paper. List them next to the letter of the sentence where you found them.

(a) While the teacher was showing us how to count, an old brown cow wandered through the group of students. (b) Even though the cow got in the way of our school work, no one did anything about it. (c) Ray did not even frown when the cow stepped on his chalk and broke it. (d) The teacher simply shouted louder over the sound of the cow's mooing. (e) You see, in India a cow is holy, and no one is allowed to disturb one. (f) The streets of our town are full of cows wandering around.

(g) At last the old brown cow lay down on the ground and went to sleep. (h) "Now may be I can learn something," I thought.

C. *oo, ou,* and *ew*

Say *zoo.* Listen for the sound of *oo.* Say *you.* Listen for the sound of *ou.* The *oo* and *ou* sound alike in these words. Say *flew.* The *ew* sounds like *oo* and *ou* in *zoo* and *you.*

1. Find a word in which *ou* sounds like *oo* in *zoo* and write it on your paper.

   rough   cough   through   thought

2. Write the word in which *oo* sounds like *ou* in *you.*

   food   door   took   good

3. Write the word in which *ew* sounds like *oo* in *zoo.*

   rewrite   reward   blew   sew

Bhondu's Lucky Day (Part III)

In this part of the story there are a number of underlined words. In some of them, *oo, ou,* and *ew* sound like the vowel sound in *zoo.* Find these words and write them on your paper in groups of *oo, ou,* and *ew* words.

At noon, when school was through for the morning, I said good-by to the group of students and started home. On my way, I stopped to see my friend Ombica. Ombica has never been to school for his father needs him to help in the fields. Few youths in my town go to school. Crops are more important than school for without them there would be nothing to eat. If you had to decide between food or education for your children, which would you choose?

I dream of the day when I can go to a real school in a big, new building. But I feel lucky just to go to any school at all. I hope that soon every child in India will have the same chance.

Critical Reading: Fact and Opinion

There are certain clues that help you to know when facts are being given. Some of these clues are numbers, names, and dates. There are some additional clues that may help you in deciding whether or not something you read is fact or a matter of opinion. These clues are phrases such as; *he says, they say, it is said, I believe,* or someone else *believes, there is a belief, I think,* or *I claim, it has been told,* and so on. All of these indicate opinion.

The opinions of other people are interesting, but often we cannot accept them as fact. If, however, an opinion is given by a specialist in a certain field, it is more apt to be worthwhile. And if an opinion is given by a majority of specialists, it may be the best information we can get.

Read the three paragraphs below, looking for the sources of the statements made. Write the answers to the questions on your own paper.

A. John Starrett is a person who is suffering from spastic paralysis. He lives in Natick, Massachusetts. Even though he walks only with a cane, he swam across the English Channel, which is 22 miles wide. This, he says, he was able to do in 12 hours and 45 minutes.

   1. What phrase gives you a clue to the source of the facts about John Starrett's swim?
   2. Do you accept this as fact?
   3. Why or why not?

B. There are light and dark areas on Mars. These areas can be seen readily when Mars is viewed through a telescope. In the past, there has been a belief among most scientists that the light areas were highlands. The dark spots were thought to be lowlands. Two scientists at the Smithsonian Observatory now have a new idea. They think that the light areas are the lowlands and that the dark areas are the highlands.

4. What is the source for the belief that the light areas are highlands?
5. What is the source for the belief that the light areas are lowlands?
6. Which source do you prefer?
7. Give reasons for your choice.

C. We would expect doctors to be very healthy people. It appears, however, that many of them are not entirely well. Tests were given to 12,000 physicians who had attended recent conventions of the American Medical Association. These tests showed that 30 percent appear to be headed for heart trouble. In addition, 30 percent had difficulties which might lead to diabetes, and 15 percent had defects which pointed toward kidney trouble.

   8. What is the source for the statement that many doctors are not entirely well?
   9. Do you accept this statement?
  10. Why or why not?

146

Practicing Fast Reading

Here is an easy selection for you to use in practicing fast reading. When you are beginning to learn to read fast, you should do most of your practice with easy stories.

You won't be able to read as fast when you are studying difficult material. But while practicing fast reading with easy material, you will get used to moving your eyes rapidly over the page. Then you probably will be able to read your study material somewhat faster also.

In reading this story, do the following:

1. Work out the pronunciation and meaning of the words at the bottom of the page.
2. Set yourself a purpose for reading the story. This will help you to read faster. Perhaps your purpose will be to find out who the characters are. It may be to find out who told the story, or what happened. It may be some other purpose. The important point is to set yourself a purpose, and keep it in mind as you read.
3. Watch the clock for an even minute. Record your beginning time. Begin at once.
4. Start reading as fast as you can. Force yourself to read faster than you have ever read before. Make your eyes leap over whole groups of words. If you find, however, that you do not get the thought, slow down a bit.

Rashid and the Lion Trainer Written by Bernadine Beatie.[4]

It was dawn. The circus tents were quiet. Rashid crept quietly into the tent that housed the caged lions and tigers. Until a month ago he had been cage boy to Hamid. He had been proud to work for Hamid, one of the best animal trainers in India.

Peela, a large yellow lioness, paced restlessly back and forth in her cage. The others animals were quiet.

"Good day!" Rashid paused at Peela's cage. The big lioness rubbed against the bars and gave a little grunt of welcome. "Ah, my pretty one, you're glad to see me."

Rashid sighed. Hamid had now bought the entire circus. He no longer had time to train the animals. He had sent for his nephew Chandra to work with the animals. Chandra had brought his own cage boy.

"Do not fret, Rashid," Hamid had said. "I shall find other jobs for you. Someday you will be back with the animals." But Rashid wondered if that someday would ever come.

"Ha! You are here again, trying to make pets of my animals," Chandra cried angrily, striding up to Rashid.

"I was just paying a friendly visit," Rashid said. "I meant no harm."

"You cannot make friends with wild animals," Chandra snapped. He poked his stick through the cage bars and gave Peela a sharp rap on the nose. "Back! Move back!" he said.

Hamid (häm′id), an animal trainer who later bought a circus

Rashid (rä′shid), a boy who helped Hamid

Chandra (shän′drə), a new animal trainer who took Hamid's place

Peela (pē′lə), the name of a lioness in the story

Peela growled deep in her throat and grabbed at the stick. Chandra struck Peela's tail. Peela moved back slowly, her eyes flaming.

"See," Chandra said. "Fear is the only thing lions and tigers understand. I do not want you to bother my animals ever again."

One morning Rashid was awakened by the sound of distant thunder. The animals would be frightened and restless. He wished that he might walk by their cages and calm them. But it would anger Chandra.

In spite of the storm, that afternoon the tent was filled with people. Rashid watched fearfully as the animals bounded into the large working cage. This working cage had been put in the center ring of the circus. Chandra stood in the middle of the cage, snapping his whip. The lions and tigers fell into place, circling the cage. The next snap of the whip signaled the animals to turn and circle in the opposite direction. But the animals did not turn.

"Turn!" Chandra ordered angrily. His whip flicked out and caught Peela's nose.

Peela whirled and banged into the side of the cage. There was a loud crash and the section of the cage Peela had hit came loose. It fell to the ground, leaving a wide gap in the cage.

"Keep your places! Remain quiet!" Rashid cried loudly. He knew that many people would be hurt if they started to run. He grabbed a chair and held it before him. Then he stepped quickly through the gap in the cage, placing his body between Peela and the frightened crowd.

"Easy, Peela. Easy, my beauty. Move back. No one will harm you." Rashid spoke soothingly and continuously. Chandra was working frantically to gain control of the other animals.

Rashid took a step forward. "Back, Peela. Back!"

Peela shook her big head. She looked at Rashid and saw who he was. Then she turned toward her stool. Rashid heard a clang as the fallen section of the cage was lifted and bolted into place.

Chandra cracked his whip, and one by one the other animals took their places.

A great cheer went up from the crowd. Hamid and Chandra lifted their hands and bowed. Then Chandra pushed Rashid forward.

"Bow!" he whispered.

Rashid bowed to left and right. The cheering increased until it was almost deafening.

Chandra grabbed Rashid by the shoulder. He said, "You, young man, you saved the day for all of us! You have taught me much this day. Now I know that my uncle's way of training is better than mine. From this very minute, you will be my assistant. You must teach me how to make friends with the animals. What do you say to that?"

Rashid was so happy that he leaped straight into the air. Then he whirled and raced toward the animal tent.

■Record Your Speed

Record your ending time. Now subtract your beginning time from your ending time. Convert your minutes into seconds and find the total number of seconds.

The number of words in the story was 700. Divide 700 by the number of seconds it took you to read the story. Then multiply by 60. The result is your speed in words per minute.

■Checking Your Understanding

To check your understanding, write on your paper "Yes" or "No" next to the number of each of these statements.

1. Before Hamid bought the circus he had been an animal trainer.

2. When Hamid bought the circus he sent for Chandra to train the animals.

3. Chandra treated Peela with kindness.

4. Very few people attended the circus because of the storm.

5. The animals did not obey Chandra when he told them to turn.

6. One of the lions caused a section of the cage to fall.

7. Rashid got Peela to go back to her stool.

8. Hamid, Chandra, and Rashid were cheered by the crowd.

9. Chandra pushed Rashid out of the tent.

10. Chandra asked Rashid to be his assistant.

Check your answers with your teacher. Give yourself a score of 10 for each correct answer. The total is your comprehension score. Compare your comprehension score and your words per minute with your previous speed reading results.

Did you make a high score in rate and a low score in comprehension? Then you had better work harder to improve your comprehension, and don't try to read so fast. Did you make a high score in comprehension but a low score in rate? Then try especially hard to improve your rate.

Working with Science Words

The words below often appear in science books and articles. If you know the meanings and pronunciations of these words, you will have less difficulty in reading and understanding your science lessons. Some of these words are probably familiar to you. Study the lesson carefully, however, to be sure that you are pronouncing them correctly and that you understand their meaning as used in science.

Study the pronunciation of each word. Say the word to yourself. Then read and think about its meaning.

diffusion (di fū′zhən), occurs when particles of one substance mix with those of another

galaxy (gal′ək sē), a universe or system in space made up of a countless number of stars

gravity (grav′ə tē), the pull that objects in space have on other objects; especially, the pull the earth has on other objects

helium (hē′lē əm), a light-weight gas, used in scientific balloons because it does not burn, as does hydrogen

humidity (hū mid′ə tē), amount of water vapor in the air

kinetic (ki net′ik), resulting from motion

nucleus (nōō′klē əs), the central part of a living cell; the central part of an atom

protein (prō′tē in), a food substance containing carbon, hydrogen, oxygen, and nitrogen; necessary for growth and repair of cells

proton (prō′ton), a tiny particle charged with positive electricity and found in the center of an atom

satellite (sat′ə līt′), a body in space, sometimes manufactured, that revolves around a larger body

Choose one of the words defined above to complete the meaning of each of these sentences. Write the correct word on your paper. You will have to add s to some of the words.

1. It is very damp and moist today. The _____ is high.

2. As a watch spring unwinds, it releases _____ energy.

3. Our sun is a star in the _____ called the Milky Way.

4. Scientists know that _____ is a safe gas to use in a balloon.

5. If ink is placed in water, the particles of ink soon mix with those of the water. This process is called _____.

6. Weather _____ are now circling the earth.

7. The _____ of an atom is split to release atomic energy.

8. _____ of an atom are charged with positive electricity.

9. If you throw a ball in the air, it comes down again. It is pulled to earth by the force of _____.

10. If we wish to keep healthy, we must eat foods containing _____.

Working with Mathematics Words

The words below appear in most mathematics textbooks at your level. Work out the pronunciation of each of the words and study the meaning that it has in mathematics. Even if you think you know the pronunciation and meaning of each word, check to make sure.

area (ãr'ē ə), the measure of a flat or curved surface, such as the number of square feet in a floor

curve (kūrv), the path passed through in going from one point to another point. These are curves:

diagonal (dī ag'ə n'l), a straight line that connects two opposite angles or corners; the line segment *AB* is a diagonal in this figure:

diminish (də min'ish), to make smaller in size or amount; when we take 2 from 8, we diminish 8 by 2

polygon (pol'ē gon), a figure having several angles and sides; these are polygons:

quadrilateral (kwäd rə lat'ẽr əl), a plane (flat) figure having four sides, such as:

pentagon (pen'tə gon), a plane figure having five sides, such as:

hexagon (hek'sə gon), a plane figure having six sides, such as:

octagon (ok'tə gon), a plane figure having eight sides, such as:

See how well you know the meaning of these words in mathematics. In some cases you are to write on your paper the word that best completes the sentence. In other cases you will be asked to draw a figure.

1. If you take away 6 from 10, you will _____ 10 by 6.

2. If you measured the top of a table and found that it was 15 square feet in size, you would be finding the _____ of the table top.

3. Draw a quadrilateral. Then draw two diagonals in it.

4. Draw three curves. Have two of them made of straight lines. Have one made of curved lines.

5. Draw a polygon having three sides.

6. Draw an octagon.

7. Draw a pentagon.

8. Draw a hexagon.

6

Wheels

HOW TO READ LITERATURE

One form of reading is really supposed to be seen and heard, not read. This form of reading is a play. A play is meant to be performed by actors before an audience. What we read on the page is meant to be used by the actors who create the performance.

Therefore, when we read a play, we have to imagine the details of what people look like, how their voices sound, what kind of place they are in. The text gives us a few clues. These clues are usually in parentheses and the letters are a different shape or size. Some plays have no clues at all—just the words that the actors will speak.

The clues in the text of a play are also a guide to the persons who create the performance. The performance may take place on different kinds of stages. Besides the actors, directors, stage designers, and costume makers may be needed. Perhaps there will be enough time and money to make very good costumes and very convincing scenery. Or the scenery and costumes may be invented in a short time and at little expense.

Reading a play instead of seeing it calls for real exercise of the imagination. Perhaps we miss much by not being able to see a performance. We miss the way talented actors use the words the author has given them. Usually we are surprised and delighted with what good actors can do with a play we have read.

On the other hand, reading a play has its advantages, too. Our imagination is free to create the performance as we wish. We can imagine scenery and costumes that are much more real than those we are ever likely to see on a stage.

The next reading gives you a chance to use your imagination. It is a play based on the real-life story of Kirkpatrick Macmillan. You may read it for all the elements you find in any story—setting, plot, characters, conflict, and theme. Try to read it also as a play, creating the performance in your head. Pay close attention to the parts in italics (type which looks like *this*) for these are the clues for your imagination to use.

Did you ever wish you could invent a new machine? Perhaps a homework-writer? A robot leaf-raker for the lawn? A bed-maker and a room-straightener? There might be quite a number of people who would buy such machines.

It's a long way between having an idea and producing a machine. And even when you have made a new machine, that is not the end of the story. You do not become a millionaire overnight. Many, many other things have to happen. The next story tells us how the bicycle had to be invented twice.

The Devil Goes to Glasgow

Written for this book
by Irene Elmer.

NARRATOR or ANNOUNCER: The first bicycle was called a hobbyhorse. It was just a wooden bar with a seat and two wheels. The hobbyhorse had handlebars to steer with, but it had no pedals. You pushed it along with your feet.

The hobbyhorse was invented in 1816. It was very popular at first. But it couldn't go fast and it couldn't go far, and it was very awkward to ride. Soon it stopped being popular. People laughed at anyone who tried to ride a hobbyhorse.

In 1840 a Scottish blacksmith named Kirkpatrick Macmillan took an old hobbyhorse and put pedals on it. The pedals hung from the handlebars. There were cranks attached to the rear axle. The cranks were joined to the pedals by long rods. When the rider swung the pedals back and forth, they turned the cranks. As the cranks turned, they made the rear wheel go around. What a contraption!

Macmillan's invention did not look like a modern bicycle, but it was a big improvement over the hobbyhorse. It could go up to 14 miles an hour. You could ride it without touching your feet to the ground, except when you wanted to start or stop. Yet Macmillan's inven-

---

contraption (kən trap'shən), any strange-looking device or machine that one does not fully understand

shilling (shil'iŋ), a silver coin of Scotland. Five shillings were worth less than $1.00

ingenious (in jēn'yəs), clever or skillful at inventing things

manufacture (man'yə fak'chər), to make goods, especially in large amounts

Michaux (mē shō'), a Frenchman who was the second person to invent the bicycle

tion never became famous. Why not? Let's go to Scotland to find out.

SCENE: *Courthill, Scotland. An early morning in 1842. Two men are leading a horse down a country road. There is a clattering noise. The men look around. Down the road comes Kirkpatrick Macmillan, riding his new invention. It has wooden wheels with iron rims that clatter on the stones of the road.*

FIRST MAN: Where are you off to, Macmillan?

(*Macmillan stops the machine by dragging both feet along the ground. The machine wobbles and almost falls over. The horse is frightened. The men quiet it.*)

MACMILLAN: I'm off to Glasgow. I'm going to give those city folk something to talk about.

FIRST MAN: You can't ride that machine to Glasgow.

SECOND MAN: It's 50 miles to Glasgow.

MACMILLAN: Fifty miles! Bah! I'll be there by noon.

FIRST MAN: If you take the stagecoach, you will.

MACMILLAN: Stagecoach! No stagecoach can keep up with me! You've seen me race the stagecoach. And who won? Who won? Tell me that! I won! Now I'm off to Glasgow to make myself famous.

FIRST MAN: You're famous here in Courthill. But city folk have never heard of you.

SECOND MAN: City folk don't care what happens in the country.

MACMILLAN: They'll care after today!

I'll show them what a country blacksmith can do! I'll be famous. You'll see.

(*Macmillan pushes the machine to start it going. Then he jumps on and goes clattering away down the road. He calls back over his shoulder*),

In Glasgow, folk will appreciate Kirkpatrick Macmillan!

FIRST MAN: What a madman!

SECOND MAN: Well, I'll take a horse, any day.

*   *   *

SCENE: *A crowded street in Glasgow at noon. There is a loud clattering noise. People look around. Down the street comes Kirkpatrick Macmillan, riding his machine. The iron-rimmed wheels make a terrible racket on the cobblestone street. Macmillan and his machine are both covered with dust. Macmillan's face is streaked with sweat and dirt.*

LADY: Heavens! What's that?

GENTLEMAN (*looks carefully at Macmillan's machine*): Why, it's a hobbyhorse. An old hobbyhorse. The kind that I rode as a boy twenty years ago. Nobody rides them nowadays. What a fool that man must be, to be riding a hobbyhorse!

LADY: It looks strange. What has he done to it?

GENTLEMAN: Oh, he's fixed it up somehow. (*Yawns*) Imagine going to all that trouble for a hobbyhorse!

(*An old woman comes to her door to see what is making so much noise. She sees Macmillan on his machine and shrieks.*)

OLD WOMAN: Oh! It's the devil! (*To her maid*) The devil has come to

Glasgow! He's out there in the street! Right out in the street he is, all covered with dirt, and riding a terrible monster with wheels!

MAID (*comes to the door*): Oh, the nasty thing! (*She shakes her broom at Macmillan*) Go away! Be off with you! (*She slams the door*)

MACMILLAN (*to himself*): Silly women. Never mind. I'll show these city folk.

(*He pedals harder. Suddenly a boy runs in front of him. Macmillan tries to stop the machine by dragging both feet along the ground, but he is going too fast. Macmillan, the boy, and the machine all fall over together with a terrible crash. Windows fly open. People shout.*)

PEOPLE: It's the devil! It's a madman! He's hit a boy! He's killed him!

Help! Police!

(*Two policemen pick up Kirkpatrick Macmillan and his machine and drag them away. The boy sits up dizzily. He shakes his head.*)

BOY: Wait till I tell my friends about this!

* * *

SCENE: *A police court that afternoon. Kirkpatrick Macmillan is standing with his machine before the judge.*

JUDGE: Well, Mr. Macmillan? What do you have to say?

MACMILLAN: It was an accident, Your Honor. My machine has no brakes.

JUDGE: I see. Did you invent this—hm—machine yourself?

MACMILLAN (*proudly*): Yes, Your Honor.

JUDGE (*examines Macmillan's machine*): Hm. Amazing. So you came to Glasgow to show off your invention?

MACMILLAN: I thought city folk would appreciate it. But they don't.

JUDGE: Mr. Macmillan, this is an amazing machine. But I want you to take it back home with you to Courthill. We city folk will be happier if you do. And you'll be happier if you do.

MACMILLAN (*crossly*): Yes, I believe I will, Your Honor. At home in Courthill, they appreciate Kirkpatrick Macmillan.

JUDGE: Now I'm going to fine you five shillings for the accident you caused. Then you may take your machine and go.

MACMILLAN (*counting five shillings out of his pocket*): Thank you, Your Honor. (*To himself*) Well, it was an expensive day, but I've learned my lesson. I'll never try to be famous again. City folks don't know a good invention when they see one.

JUDGE: Just one more thing, Mr. Macmillan. This is—hm—a very interesting machine. Very interesting and ingenious. I want you to know that the Court appreciates your talent. The Court would like to offer you these five shillings as a small tribute to your creativity.

(*Looking very serious, the judge gives the five shillings back to Macmillan. Macmillan takes them. He grins broadly.*)

You may go home now, Mr. Macmillan. Case dismissed.

MACMILLAN: Thank you, Your Honor.

(*Still grinning broadly, he takes his machine and goes. The iron-rimmed wheels clatter noisily down the street as Kirkpatrick Macmillan rides his invention home.*)

NARRATOR or ANNOUNCER: Kirkpatrick Macmillan never tried to manufacture his invention. In a few years, people had forgotten it. But in 1861 a bicycle with pedals was invented again. The inventor lived in Paris, France. His name was Ernest Michaux. Michaux's machine had brakes. By now people had forgotten the old-fashioned hobbyhorse; so no one laughed at Michaux's invention. He decided to manufacture it, and that is how the bicycle industry began.

ACTIVITY 1 — Fact Questions

1. What is a hobbyhorse?

2. Where does the story take place?

3. In what century does it take place?

4. What did Kirkpatrick Macmillan do for a living?

5. What town did he live in?

6. How far did he ride to Glasgow?

7. How had his appearance changed by the time he got to Glasgow?

8. Why did the policemen take him to court?

9. What was Macmillan's fine?

10. What did he decide to do about his new invention?

2 ACTIVITY — Thought Questions

1. Why do you think the hobbyhorse was popular at first?

2. Why did Macmillan's machine make so much noise?

3. How did the machine affect horses?

4. Why did the old woman think Macmillan was a devil?

5. What important part of a bicycle did Macmillan's machine lack?

6. How do you think the judge felt about Macmillan's invention?

7. Why do you think Macmillan never manufactured his machine?

8. Why do you think Michaux had better luck with his invention than Macmillan?

---

3 ACTIVITY — Understanding Plays

In Column I are some clues from the play. In Column II are some things made or done by performers, designers, or others who help produce a play. Match the clue on the left with the action or thing most closely associated with it on the right. Write the number of the clue and the letter of the action or thing on your paper.

I	II
1. Scene: a crowded street in Glasgow	A. The kind of broom used in the 19th century is found or made.
2. Scene: a police court in Scotland in 1842. Macmillan is standing before the judge.	B. Burnt cork or very dark makeup is placed where the actor who plays Macmillan can quickly use it between scenes.
3. Macmillan's face is covered with sweat and dirt.	C. Scenery showing doors and windows of town houses lining a street is built and painted.
4. Maid shakes her broom at Macmillan.	D. Records describing Macmillan's machine are studied and something similar to it is built.
5. Down the road comes Kirkpatrick Macmillan, riding his new invention.	E. Costumes appropriate for a country man and a judge in Scotland of the 1840's are sewn.

**HOW TO READ IN
SOCIAL STUDIES**

Often your aim in reading in social studies is to solve problems. The problems that concern us now have their roots in the past. For that reason, history is a part of social studies. To understand a problem fully, we must grasp facts and relate them to each other. One way to grasp and relate facts is to find a pattern for them. Cause-effect and compare-contrast are two of these patterns. Solving problems in a society also means that we must understand people. For this reason, social studies includes a bit of psychology, too.

There may be many possible solutions to a problem. Sometimes we have to try them, one after another. Sometimes only by studying failure can we arrive at success. A problem-solver must be ready to move off in any direction. He must go where his reasoning and his judgment direct.

In reading the next article, you will be a problem-solver. You will be given some history of a problem, many facts, and some patterns. Your job is to think of solutions.

As you read, look for facts. Look for the patterns of cause-and-effect or compare-contrast that organize these facts. Look also for attempted or suggested solutions.

How fast things changed after Macmillan's time! Once we got moving, it seems we kept going faster and faster. Shortly after bicycles came locomotives, then automobiles, and then airplanes. The inventions we have now would take Macmillan's breath away.

Yet in some ways we are not really moving as fast as we think we are. A critic of our postal system once carried a letter by horse across New York City. Even at a comfortable clip-clop, he was faster than the postal service. People who are stuck for hours in traffic jams or in stalled railroad cars often wonder if these inventions really add to their lives. Perhaps instead they subtract from their lives in hours lost, irritation, and expense. What do you think? Is "progress" real? Read on for facts to form your own opinion.

Super Cities — Tangled Transport

Written for this book
by Joseph Dempsey.

A megalopolis is a super city made up of many cities. One megalopolis in the United States includes the giant cities of Boston, New York, Philadelphia, Baltimore, and Washington, along with smaller cities and suburban towns. In that megalopolis, 20% of the American people live on 1.4% of the nation's land.

Another megalopolis seems to be building up south of the Great Lakes between Chicago, Pittsburgh, and Detroit. A third may be gathering along the

megalopolis (meg'ə lop'ə lis), vast, continuously urban area

electromagnetic (i lek'trō mag net'ik), produced by an electromagnet, or iron which temporarily becomes a magnet when an electric current goes through a coil around it

California coast as the suburbs of San Francisco and Los Angeles expand.

The people who live in a megalopolis are constantly on the move. Trains, buses, subways, airplanes, but mostly cars, whisk them from one place to another.

Transportation within the super city is a serious problem. So many people are moving about on the roads and in the air that quite often they all jam together. More and more cars are made and bought each year. About 8,000,000 new cars are produced yearly and 5,000,000 cars are scrapped. As a result, there are 22 cars for every mile of road.

Another part of the transportation

problem is air pollution. Fumes from automobiles are said to be the worst offenders in air pollution. For some people with lung disorders, air pollution can cause illness and even death. It has been proved that air that is overloaded with pollutants endangers everybody's health.

Some cities monitor the air every day and issue warnings when the pollution is at a dangerous level. Others outlaw the sale of certain kinds of gas. Still other laws call for exhaust controls on car engines.

These solutions are incomplete. Few people can stay out of the city when pollution is high. They have to go to work. Controls are not state-wide. Many people vote down any law that results in higher prices on cars or gas — even when their health would benefit.

What else can be done? Some experts say that the solution is the development of more and better trains. They point out it takes nine times as much space for one person to travel by car as by bus or train. Better public transport to take workers back and forth between their homes in the suburbs and their jobs in the city can help. Experts also want to build large jet-ports away from the city with a monorail connection to the train stations.

The Japanese have developed the fastest passenger train. Their Tokaido Express runs between Tokyo and Osaka, a distance of 320 miles. The train averages 125 miles per hour and completes the trip with two stops in less than three hours.

The Japanese also have in service a high-speed monorail train. This train goes from Tokyo International Airport to downtown Tokyo, a distance of 8 miles, in 15 minutes. A car in heavy traffic usually takes an hour.

The French have developed the Aerotrain. It moves on a cushion of air along a steel track at 300 miles per hour. The British have developed a similar train called the Hovertrain. Both are powered by noiseless and pollution-free motors.

The Germans have developed a train they named the Levitrain. It is a magnetic suspension vehicle using electromagnetic forces to keep it a little bit above a guide track. The air-cushion and magnetic suspension trains can move very fast because they do not come in contact with a surface as do the wheels of a car or a regular train.

Why is America behind these other countries in rapid-train development? Some experts believe it is because Americans have fallen in love with cars. They say that the car is a symbol of success to an American. Given a choice of private or public transport, the average American prefers to go in the car rather than take a bus or train.

These experts believe that the United States will not make headway on the transportation problem until Americans fall out of love with their cars.

There are ways to discourage people from using their cars in the city. High tolls could be placed on highways, bridges, and tunnels going into the city. High parking fees might also help to discourage car owners.

Americans have a lot to think about if they are to survive in a megalopolis. Can you think of other solutions to these problems?

Above—exhaust fumes and pollutants from a bus in New York City; below—express train in Tokyo.

The problem in the previous article has many and complicated causes. Some of the events or situations that contribute to the problem are described in the first part of each statement below. Read each statement and select the best cause to complete the statement. Write the number of the statement and the letter of the cause on your paper.

1. Transportation in a megalopolis has become a problem because
   a. more people live more closely together than in other areas.
   b. more people need cars than in other areas.
   c. there is less public transport than in other areas.

2. The air pollution problem is connected to the transportation problem because
   a. new trains have been invented in other countries.
   b. Aerotrain, Hovertrain, and Levi-train do not touch the ground while moving.
   c. fumes from auto engines are an important part of air pollution.

3. There are now 22 cars per mile of road because
   a. we have not built new roads.
   b. we produce more new cars than we scrap every year.
   c. roads are overcrowded.

4. Buses and trains can save space because
   a. newly invented trains are pollution-free.
   b. a person who commutes in a car takes up nine times as much space as a person who commutes in a train or bus.
   c. we have airplanes which fly three times faster than sound.

5. Other countries have improved public transport faster than we have probably because
   a. they needed their public transport more.
   b. they have not spent enough money on research.
   c. our research is better.

Here are three main ideas which you might use to outline the article on transportation. Choose from the list those statements which may be details or parts of each main idea. Note that each main-idea statement gives you a clue to the number of details to select for it. Write the Roman numeral of the main idea on your paper and the Arabic numerals of the details which go with it.

I. Three areas in the U.S. have become super cities in recent years.

II. The increasing number of passenger cars creates two problems.

164

III. Foreign countries are solving this problem faster than we are, as shown by five examples of newly invented foreign trains.

1. The Germans have developed the Levitrain, which is a magnetic suspension vehicle.

2. The first problem is that our ground transport is frequently traffic-jammed.

3. Boston, New York, Philadelphia, Baltimore, and Washington are part of one big megalopolis.

4. Hovertrain, developed by the British, is noiseless and pollution-free.

5. France has the new air-cushion train named the Aerotrain.

6. Another problem is air pollution.

7. The fastest passenger train is the Tokaido Express between Tokyo and Osaka.

8. South of the Greak Lakes another megalopolis may be building up.

9. The Japanese have developed a high-speed monorail between Tokyo International Airport and downtown Tokyo.

10. A third megalopolis may be gathering along the California coast.

HOW TO READ IN SCIENCE

Science books and social studies books often give causes and effects. You are given the causes of certain things which happen, and you are told the effects, or results, of these causes.

The next article is like the parts in your science books that explain causes and effects of certain things. If you read carefully to find what the different causes are and what effect each cause has, you are more likely to understand the material.

Read the article with two purposes in mind: (a) to understand why something happened; in other words, the *cause* of each effect; (b) to understand what happens; in other words, the *effects* of each cause.

Then do Activity 1. This checks your understanding of causes and effects. Try to do well in this activity, because finding causes and effects is a very important skill.

There were some dangers connected with Macmillan's machine. One was the danger of running into someone. Without brakes, there was also danger to the rider if he went too fast down a hill. Another danger was the effect the machine might have on horses.

However, these dangers were small compared to the dangers of modern transport. Read on to find out the risks we take in order to move faster and more comfortably.

The Whys and Hows of Air Pollution

Written for this book by Leonard Bernstein.

Many people think that the Space Age began with the invention of the rocket engine. Some people may say that it started when a paper clip was first launched by a rubber band. Perhaps it really began when humans lifted their heads and looked at the stars. No one knows for sure. But one thing is certain. From early times, men and women have searched for new ways to move themselves and their belongings.

The sled, wheel, and raft were probably among the earliest inventions of human beings. Each had an influence on human life. Most people would say that that influence was for the better.

carbon monoxide (kär′bən mon ok′sīd), colorless, odorless, highly poisonous gas

nitrogen oxide (nī′trə jən ok′sīd), a gas which causes the formation of smog

sulfur (sul′fēr), a yellow chemical element that burns with a stifling odor

But what about the more modern methods of transportation? What about trains, planes, automobiles, and ships? Think of the effects these have on our everyday life. They influence the foods we eat, the clothes we wear, and even where we live. But is it for the better?

There is one effect of modern ways of transport that is not for the better. This is the invisible but deadly effect of pollution. Pollution is anything added to the environment that is harmful to living things.

Moving from one place to another means using energy. Energy means burning fuels. And burning fuels usually means pollution. There are many different kinds of pollution. Each kind of pollution is harmful to living things in one way or another.

The automobile is often described as a major source of air pollution. Many automobile manufacturers argue that this is not true. Yet the statistics are staggering. There are more than 100 million automobiles in the United States. They account for more than 60% of our air pollution.

In 1972, the U.S. used approximately 80 billion gallons of gasoline. Each gallon of gasoline produces about three pounds of carbon monoxide, a very deadly gas. Simple arithmetic shows that about 120 million tons of carbon monoxide were added to the air we breathed that year. Nitrogen oxide is a gas which causes the formation of smog. Five million tons of this gas were

Pollutant	Major Source	Effect
Carbon monoxide	Automobile engines produce about 85% of this gas.	Reduces oxygen intake. Produces nausea, dizziness, and death from excess
Nitrogen oxide	Automobile and diesel engines	Irritates eyes, nose, bronchial tubes and lungs. Triggers reaction causing smog. High concentrations can cause death
Lead	Leaded gasoline	Affects the nervous system and is harmful to red blood cells. May cause heart disease and death
Nickel	Added to gasoline to prevent knock	Can cause cancer of nasal passages and lungs
Asbestos	Used in brake linings of automobiles and trucks	May cause respiratory disease and lung cancer

added to the atmosphere by automobile engines.

Let's not forget the wheel. Modern automobile and truck tires are made of rubber to which sulfur has been added for extra strength. As rubber tires spin at high speeds, they wear down. Almost 3 billion pounds of rubber dust and 100 million pounds of sulfur particles must be added to the list of pollutants resulting from automobiles. To help the engines run smoothly and quietly, lead or nickel are added to gasoline. Too much of either of these in the air can cause death. Look at the chart to find out what these pollutants can do to you.

Air pollution is not the only hazard of modern transportation. Along with heavy truck loads and fast speeds comes noise—lots of it. Noise pollution is a serious problem. And it's getting worse. The amount of noise in the United States is doubling every 10 years. Some of the major causes of noise pollution are jet planes, motorcycles, trains, and trucks. Motorboats, snowmobiles, and sports cars also contribute their share. You don't think noise can hurt you? Noise can cause hearing loss, ulcers, and "nerves." It's another one of the prices we pay for modern transportation. But the price has become very high, perhaps too high. Are we going to continue to pay it? Transportation was designed to help human beings. In many ways, it does. But has it begun to threaten us?

ACTIVITY 1

Answer these questions on your paper.

1. The automobile is often described as a major source of air pollution. Tell why.

2. Rubber particles are added to the atmosphere. Name one cause.

3. Over 120 million tons of carbon monoxide gas are added to the air we breathe. Name one cause.

4. Smog is a condition of the atmos-phere. What is one of its chief causes?

5. What is the effect on the human body of carbon monoxide in the at-mosphere?

6. What is one cause for the appear-ance of asbestos fibers in the at-mosphere?

7. What effect can asbestos fibers in the air have on people?

8. What is the effect of lead or nickel on automobile engines?

9. What is the effect of lead or nickel on people?

10. What is one major cause of noise pollution?

11. What are some effects of noise pol-lution?

An Experiment to Study Pollution _____

In the next paragraphs you will find directions for performing an experiment. In working with this kind of material, you should read each direction separately and think about it. You must read every word carefully, making sure that you understand each one. Then you must carry out the directions exactly.

For this experiment we have shown you pictures of what happened when we performed the steps. Read each set of directions as if you were going to carry out the directions. Then think through the answers to the questions.

Finally if possible, carry out the steps yourself and record your results.

You can perform a simple experi-ment to study pollution in your area. You need only some glass slides, some petroleum jelly, and a strong magnify-ing glass. If your school has a micro-scope, that would be even better than a magnifying glass.

Before you begin your experiment,

decide what place you want to test. It could be a closet, your classroom, your home, or play area. You may want to compare inside air with outside air. Whatever place you choose, you need other places for comparison. Choose at least two other places. For our experiment, we chose a place where we thought pollution would be bad—a spot near a busy highway. Our second was a place we thought would be clean —green fields on a hilltop.

Step 1: Paste a label or write a number on the back of each slide so that you can identify it later. On the other side apply a thin coating of petroleum jelly. You may use the edge of another slide to spread the jelly evenly. Be sure to cover the whole slide.

Step 2: Set one slide, coated side up, in the place to be tested. Set your other slides in their places. Do not cover the slides. Do not disturb them for two days.

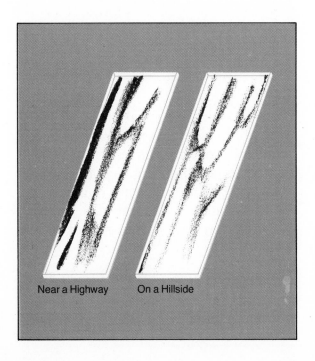

Near a Highway   On a Hillside

Step 3: After two days, carefully examine each of your slides. Use the magnifying glass or microscope to count all of the particles stuck to the jelly. Here are our two slides after two days.

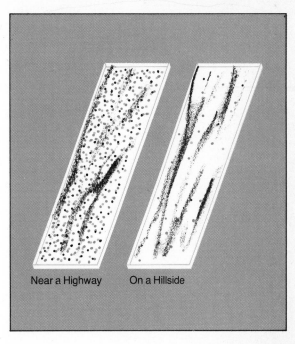

Near a Highway   On a Hillside

Answer these questions on your paper.

a. Which slide has more particles?
b. Which slide has fewer particles?
c. Why do you think one slide has fewer particles than the other?

HOW TO READ IN MATHEMATICS

When you read a social studies article discussing problems, you often find information given in percentages. You may read that ten percent of the population of a city owns a certain kind of bicycle.

Since you read percentages often, it is important that you know what is meant by *percent*. Percent is simply another name for one type of fraction numeral. In this lesson you will work with fraction numerals and see how they are related to the meaning of percent.

Some people hope that the bicycle, which was one of the first inventions of modern transport, may help save it. The bicycle burns no fuel and takes up little road space. It slips through traffic jams and takes up very little room in a parking lot. For short distances in a city, it can be much faster than a car, taxi, or bus.

Sales of bicycles are soaring, as people do more bike-riding to commute as well as to have fun. Recently, the number of bicycles in use was estimated to be 65,000,000. This was nearly 70 percent of the number of passenger cars in use. In addition, about 50 percent of the bicycles sold these days are for adults. Do these statistics show that the bicycle can ease the transportation problem?

In trying to solve problems, a percent is often an important statistic. Read on to find out more about percent.

The Meaning of Percent _____

Written for this book
by William L. Schaaf.

Percent is a useful way to show comparisons. You are probably familiar with one way of showing comparisons. If you wanted to compare four peanuts to five peanuts, you could write the comparison like this: 4 to 5, or 4:5, or $\frac{4}{5}$.

Notice that this comparison is shown by a fraction numeral. A fraction numeral which is used to show a com-

parison is called a ratio. The ratio $\frac{4}{5}$ does not have to mean four-fifths of one whole. It does not have to mean four-fifths of one group. It means that we are comparing 4 to 5. We are comparing a set of 4 peanuts to a set of 5 peanuts. We are comparing at the rate of 4 to 5.

1. On your paper, write ratios to show the following comparisons.
   a. 3 hot dogs compared to 10 hot dogs.

_____

ratio (rā'shē ō), a fixed relation between two similar things, often expressed as a fraction

b. 6 out of 20 astronauts

c. 9 cars in each 50

d. 1 sprinter out of 25 sprinters

e. 50 out of 100 umpires

f. 19 people out of 20 people

Look at the ratio you wrote for (e). The correct ratio is $\frac{50}{100}$. This ratio may be called 50 percent.

Here are some more ratios written also as percents.

$\frac{6}{100}$ or 6 percent

$\frac{25}{100}$ or 25 percent

$\frac{72}{100}$ or 72 percent

$\frac{99}{100}$ or 99 percent

$\frac{100}{100}$ or 100 percent

$\frac{300}{100}$ or 300 percent

We call the numerals in a ratio the *terms* of the ratio. The numeral above the line is the *first term* of the ratio. The numeral below the line is the *second term* of the ratio.

$\frac{4}{5}$ (first term)
(second term)

Did you see that in each of the ratios shown above, the second term is 100? When any ratio has 100 as its second term, it may be called a percent. Thus, $\frac{65}{100}$ is 65 percent; $\frac{90}{100}$ is 90 percent; and $\frac{32}{100}$ is 32 percent.

2. a. Write $\frac{20}{100}$ as a percent.

   b. Write $\frac{85}{100}$ as a percent.

   c. Write $\frac{35}{100}$ as a percent.

We use this sign % to stand for percent. We may write 60 percent, or 60%. We may write 100 percent, or 100%. It may be helpful for you to think of the "zeros" in the percent sign as the two zeros in the numeral 100.

Write each of the following ratios as a percent, using the percent sign.

3. a. $\frac{45}{100}$ **e.** $\frac{28}{100}$

   b. $\frac{100}{100}$ **f.** $\frac{89}{100}$

   c. $\frac{1}{100}$ **g.** $\frac{76}{100}$

   d. $\frac{13}{100}$ **h.** $\frac{33}{100}$

4. Write each of the following percentages as ratios. Use 100 as the second term of the ratio.

   a. 15% **d.** 2%

   b. 96% **e.** 24%

   c. 125% **f.** 31%

   g. 65%

1
ACTIVITY

1. In Denmark 50 out of 100 people own bicycles. What percent of the people own bicycles?

2. In the world about 6% of the people own telephones. Out of every 100 people, about how many own telephones?

3. About 98% of the people in our town go to church. Out of every 100 people in our town, about how many go to church?

4. On Friday 85% of Joe's class was present. Were any of the students absent? What percent?

5. One day Louise noticed that sixty boys were wearing long-sleeve shirts, and forty were wearing short-sleeve shirts. What percent of the total number of boys were wearing long-sleeve shirts?

Organizing Sentences into Paragraphs _____

Below you will find several sentences about two topics that have to do with transportation. These sentences are not organized into paragraphs. That is for you to do. If you do some organizing of sentences into paragraphs yourself, you will find it easier to read paragraphs that other people have written.

The topic of each of the paragraphs is given in one of the boxes. There are several sentences that belong to each topic. On your paper, make two columns headed 1. The Beginning of the Railroad and 2. Highways of the Future. Under each heading write the letters of the sentences that belong to that topic.

> **1.** The Beginning of the Railroad
>
> **2.** Highways of the Future

(a) You would not have to watch the road because the highway would take over the driving.

(b) But the locomotive could move several times faster than a horse and pull far heavier loads.

(c) Until the train was invented, no one had ever traveled faster than a horse.

(d) Electric highways may be the best way to solve today's traffic problems.

(e) The steam locomotive changed human life.

(f) Even our eating habits began to change because of the railroad.

(g) People began to travel on trains, to move about more, and to build new cities.

(h) An electric rail built into the road would pull the car along.

(i) Cars could go faster and travel closer together; so more cars would fit on the roads.

(j) This sounds surprising, but it may happen in the near future.

■ Finding the Main Idea and Details

1. Look at the sentences you grouped with "The Beginning of the Railroad." Which one gives the main idea of a paragraph?

2. Look at the sentences you grouped with "Highways of the Future." Which one gives the main idea of a paragraph?

3. Now see if you can arrange the sentences for each paragraph in their proper order. Reread all the sentences in your first group. On your paper, write a well-organized paragraph using all of these sentences. Start with the main idea. Then pay attention to the order of things as they happen in time. Do the same thing with your second group of sentences. Remember to give your paragraph a title.

More Practice in Fast Reading

You have had practice in trying to read two stories fast. You will now have one more chance to try reading a story fast. You may then compare your rates in reading these three stories and see if you have improved. Record your beginning time and start to read.

This story is true and interesting. Exciting things happen one after another. You will want to read it fast because you will be curious to know what happened.

◼ A Giant Seesaw   Written by Clare Thorne.[5]

The flatboat was stranded.

A tall, gawky young man stood trying to figure out a way to get it over the dam on which it was stuck. Since yesterday he and the rest of the flatboat crew had been trying to push the boat loose.

As they pushed, the young man could hear the laughter and loud voices of the crowd that had gathered to watch from the riverbank. It seemed as though the whole village of New Salem had gathered there.

"That boat is stuck as fast as a burr in a buffalo hide," yelled someone in the crowd. "They won't get it off till next time the river floods."

"The way that boat is taking on water, I'll bet you a dollar it sinks before they can work it loose," someone else said.

"I'll take that bet," another answered. "My dollar is on that young fellow who's telling the crew what to do. He's so tall, he can't get his breeches to cover his ankles! Why, tall as he is, he could jump in, stand on the bottom, and push the boat free!"

It was hard to be laughed at, even though the tall young man knew that the laughter was not meant to be mean. But so much depended on the success of this trip.

He had been hired to pilot the flatboat down the river. This was his first real job. He was on his own, out to make his way in the world. The owner of this flatboat was the first person to show enough confidence in him to treat him like a grown man. More than anything else he wanted to live up to that confidence.

But here, right at the start of the journey, he had made a mistake that might ruin everything.

When they came round the bend yesterday, they saw the low dam that stretched across the river. They should have used their poles to slow the flatboat down. Instead, they tried to get up speed and slide over the dam.

It didn't work. Before they were halfway over the dam, there was an awful scrape and thud. The boat jolted to a stop. Then the front end tilted up and the back end down.

To make matters worse, the cargo—barrels of salt pork, sacks of dry corn, and a half dozen live hogs—slid to the back of the boat. That weighed it down even more. The back of the boat sank deeper. Water started spilling into the boat!

All their pushing couldn't budge the boat. Now, if something wasn't done soon, the boat would start sinking.

Scratching his head thoughtfully, the tall young man tried to decide what to do.

"I should have eased her up to the dam as gentle as a mother with a new baby!" he said to himself. "Then, when she scraped, we could have shifted the weight forward and tilted her across."

Tilted her across!

Why hadn't he thought of that before? For a whole day and a night he had been straining his muscles. Why hadn't he used his head as well?

"Look here, boys, I've got an idea," he said to his crewmates. "Let's lighten the load a little. Unload the pork barrels!"

"We got nothing to unload into," one of the boys said.

"Just heave the barrels over the side," the young man said. "They'll float, and the dam will keep them from getting away."

So one after the other, the heavy barrels were lifted out of the boat and rolled overboard with a splash.

The crowd gasped when they saw how strong the young man was. He rolled a barrel and pushed it over in the same amount of time it took for the other two men to do the same thing, working together.

Soon the boat was emptied of everything but the water and the tied-up hogs. All three of the flatboatmen stood in the front of the boat. When their weight equalled the weight in the back, the boat began to tilt forward.

But it was tilting too fast! The flatboat was balancing on the dam like a giant seesaw!

As the front end tipped over the dam, the water in the back of the boat surged forward. The three young men had to jump to the center of the boat to keep it from turning end over end.

And then, just when they thought they had it balanced, the hogs came sliding forward, snorting and splashing and drenching the three young men as they passed.

The crowd on the riverbank laughed till their sides hurt. This was better than a circus.

But the tall young man wasn't paying any attention to the onlookers. He moved calmly toward the back of the boat to balance the weight of the hogs. Soon the boat was balanced across the low dam with one end sticking over the edge.

"You have to hand it to that young feller," someone shouted. "He's got a cool head."

"It'll have to be even cooler to get that boat over in one piece," someone else said. "He's got to get rid of the water to lighten the load. It'll take him a week to bail the boat dry."

But the gawky young man had put his cool head to work on that, too.

"Anybody hereabouts got anything I could use to drill a hole?" he shouted in a loud cheerful voice.

A boy, who was fishing from the dam, spoke up, "Henry Onstot's got a tool for making holes in his barrels."

"Reckon you could show me where to find him?" the tall young man asked.

"Sure," the boy answered. He used his fishing pole to point out Henry Onstot's store.

The tall young man went to borrow the tool and was soon back and ready to work. He made his way to the front of the boat, knelt down, and started drilling a hole. A minute or so later, he straightened up, gave the tool back to the boy, and sat down to whittle a plug of soft wood.

The crowd on the bank applauded as they realized what the young man was doing. There was a little stream of water running out of the end of the boat that hung over the dam. The boat was bailing itself without any effort on his part. It began to tilt gently forward.

Soon the boat was dry. The young man plugged up the hole with the wood he had whittled. Then he and his companions eased the boat over the dam.

The problem was solved.

The owner of the boat had been watching very quietly from the riverbank. Now he spoke.

"I tell you that young fellow is going to amount to something," he boasted. "He's the smartest man in this part of Illinois! He's smart enough to be president someday! Mark my words!"

The crowd roared with laughter.

"Give me a hand, Abe," said the boat-owner to the tall young man.

Abraham Lincoln helped his employer board the flatboat, and they floated down the river.

Record Your Speed

Record your ending time. Now figure out your words per minute. Subtract your beginning time from your ending time. The answer will be in minutes and seconds. Convert your answer into seconds. There were 1175 words in this story. Divide the number of words by your total reading time in seconds. Multiply the result by 60. Now you have your words per minute.

Check Your Understanding

Answer "yes" or "no" to each of the statements below on your own paper.

1. The flatboat had been stuck for a day.

2. The tall young man was the leader of a crew of four.

3. Piloting the flatboat was his first real job.

4. He had made the right decision to speed up to slide over the dam.

5. The back of the flatboat was weighed down with barrels, sacks, and live hogs.

6. Water spilled into the boat and the boat threatened to sink.

7. The boat tilted forward too fast when all the crew stood in the back.

8. The boy with the fishing pole borrowed a tool for the tall young man.

9. The water drained out of the boat through a hole the young man drilled.

10. Everybody laughed when the boat-owner said Abraham Lincoln was smart enough to be president.

Check your answers with your teacher. Give yourself 10 points for each correct answer. The total is your comprehension score.

Now compare the scores you made in reading the three stories. Did you improve in rate? Did you improve in comprehension, lose in comprehension, or stay the same?

Working with Words Opposite in Meaning _____

After each pair of sentences, there are three words in parentheses. Choose the word that is opposite in meaning to the underlined word in the first sentence of each pair. The word you choose will complete the second sentence. Write and number the words on your own paper.

1. This isn't the <u>ending</u>. It's the _____. (last, start, way)
2. You must do the <u>whole</u> thing, not a _____. (part, past, day)
3. Don't look <u>up</u>. Look _____. (over, in, down)
4. Try to <u>smile</u>, not to _____. (grin, frown, win)
5. Don't do it <u>wrong</u>. Do it _____. (left, right, tall)
6. The room's not <u>dark</u>. The room is _____. (big, small, bright)
7. I'm not over <u>there</u>. I'm over _____. (here, head, turned)
8. I'm not <u>far</u>, I'm _____. (near, lost, burned)
9. Ned is <u>happy</u>. He's not _____. (glad, sad, mad)
10. Ted is <u>good</u>. He's not _____. (bad, mad, glad)
11. That car's not <u>rapid</u>. It's _____. (quick, fast, slow)
12. That star's not <u>high</u>. It's _____. (blow, low, last)
13. Bob doesn't <u>push</u>. He has to _____. (wait, pull, shove)
14. The room's not <u>empty</u>. It's _____. (straight, quiet, full)
15. The room's not full of <u>girls</u>. It's full of _____. (people, hair, boys)
16. It's not full of <u>silence</u>. It's full of _____. (noise, air, people)
17. Dan lives in the <u>country</u>, not the _____. (farm, street, city)
18. Jan isn't <u>ugly</u>. She is _____. (small, neat, pretty)
19. The road's not <u>curved</u>. It's _____. (hard, last, straight)
20. Fred's not <u>early</u>. He's _____. (happy, fast, late)
21. Mack's not <u>short</u>. He's _____. (nice, small, tall)
22. Jack's not <u>huge</u>. He's _____. (big, small, tall)
23. The day's not <u>dry</u>. It's _____. (cold, hot, wet)
24. I can't <u>remember</u>. I _____. (wonder, forget, not)
25. I am not your <u>enemy</u>. I'm your _____. (mother, friend, teacher)
26. This is not the <u>beginning</u>. It's the _____! (stop, end, start)

Reviewing Silent Consonants

Consonants in a word are often silent. There are no hard-and-fast guides for all silent consonants. There are a few guides, however, that hold true in most cases. On this page you will have a chance to work with these guides. Answer the questions on your paper and choose the correct word or letter within the parentheses to complete each guide.

A. 1. Say these words: *knee, knife, knob, know.* Did you hear the *k* in any of these words?

2. What letter came after *k* in each word?

3. Complete this guide:

   Guide 1: When *k* comes at the beginning of a word and is followed by *n* the (*k, n*) is usually silent.

4. Say these words: *comb, lamb, climb, limb.* Did you hear the *b* in any of these words?

5. What letter did *b* follow in each word?

6. Complete this guide:

   Guide 2: When *b* follows *m* at the end of a word, (*b, m*) is usually silent.

7. Say these words: *wrong, wrinkle, write, wrap.* Did you hear the *w* in any of these words?

8. What letter followed *w*?

9. Complete this guide:

   Guide 3: When *w* is followed by *r*, the (*w, r*) is silent.

10. Say these words: *half, calf, walk, yolk.* Did you hear the *l* in any of these words?

11. What letter came after *l* in the first two words?

12. What letter came after *l* in the last two words?

13. Complete this guide:

   Guide 4: When *l* comes before *f* or *k* it is usually (silent, sounded).

14. Say these words: *fight, light, right, might.* Did you hear the *gh* in these words?

15. What letter follows *gh* in each word?

16. Is the *i* in each word long or short?

17. Complete this guide:

   Guide 5: When the letters *gh* follow *i*, *gh* is (silent, sounded) and the *i* has the long sound.

18. Say these words: *catch, pitch, notch, hatch.* Did you hear the *t* in these words?

19. How many syllables were in each word?

20. Where did the *t* come in the word?

21. Complete this guide:

   Guide 6: When the letter *t* is in the middle of a one-syllable word, ending in *ch*, the (*t, ch*) is silent.

B. What did Bill think when his car broke down for the tenth time: To find out, follow these directions:

1. Copy these letters and blanks on your paper:

   _ i _ _ _ hou _ _ _ i _ _ ou _ d _ e _ es _ _ o _ a _ _ .

2. Write the numbers from 1 to 16 on your paper.

3. One of the words in each pair below has silent letters. The other does not. On your paper, write the word that has one or more silent letters.

4. Circle the silent letters.

5. After you have circled all the silent letters, write them in order in the blanks to finish the sentence.

1. dumb — dancer
2. tablet — talk
3. half — hats
4. hitch — hurt
5. best — bright

6. twig — batch
7. notch — next
8. wren — went
9. chin — chalk
10. numb — never

11. crest — crumb
12. witch — west
13. watch — water
14. wreath — windy
15. casting — calf
16. kids — kneel

7

Input/Output

Now that you know the elements of a story, let's look a little more closely at *theme*. The theme is the main idea of a story. Sometimes it is clear. Sometimes it is not stated directly. But it is repeated or hinted at many times in a story. The title of a story is an important clue to the theme.

The theme usually involves the main character in a story and what the experiences of the story meant to him or to her. We all have similar experiences in life. We have similar thoughts and feelings, too. We come to some of the same conclusions. So the theme of a story is often a thought that might apply to many people. For instance, the conquest of Everest meant for Tensing a conquest of his own fear and his own physical limitations. Many other kinds of struggles might have the same theme.

When we state a theme, there is much that we leave out. The theme is a summing-up of the whole experience. It is not each event, one by one. But by looking at each event one by one we can see the theme. For instance, in Tensing's story, there were many occasions when he was afraid, when he was in danger, when he was straining himself to his limits. *All* these events are *summed up* by the theme—conquest of fear, conquest of physical limits.

In the next story, look also for a repetition of events and feelings. Look at all the different ways the story shows Consuela disliking computers. Look for what the events mean to her. At the same time, be aware of character, conflict, setting, and plot.

Did you ever get the feeling that machines are smarter than we are? If you've ever watched an adding machine clicking out sums, you might feel outclassed. A speeding motorist who has been caught in a highway speed trap can be helplessly enraged at radar. A bank robber identified by a photo taken by automatic cameras has also been outsmarted—and by something not totally human.

The increasing use of machines in our lives makes many people uneasy. The next story tells us about a girl who felt that way—and the surprising thing that happened to her.

A Trip to the Computer _____

Written for this book
by Juliana O. Muehrcke.

"Still studying? Don't you ever get sick of it?"

Consuela was sitting reading a book. She looked up to find Luis Perez standing there.

"I'm not studying," she said. "I'm reading for the fun of it."

A look of surprise crossed Luis' face. Reading was the last thing he would choose to do for fun. In his spare time Luis worked as a computer programmer. That was Consuela's idea of total boredom. On the other hand, Luis thought she was crazy to enjoy writing for the school paper.

Consuela set her book aside, wishing she could finish reading it instead of having to spend the afternoon with Luis Perez. In fact, she would rather do anything than spend the day with him. "Aren't you early, Luis?" she asked.

"I'm right on time," Luis said. He held his watch in front of Consuela's face to prove his point. It was exactly one o'clock.

"Of course, Luis would arrive on the

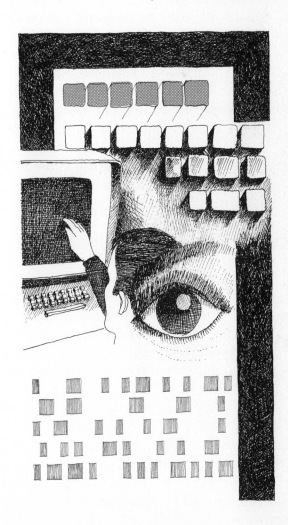

dot," Consuela thought with annoyance. He was like a computer, never making mistakes. She and Luis were as opposite as two people could be, and they would never get along. She wouldn't be with him now if she didn't have to be. But Consuela had been asked to write a story for the school paper about Luis' work on the computer. There was no way to get out of it.

Consuela sighed as she got up. She might as well get it over with.

As they walked toward the computer center, Luis chattered eagerly about computers. "Did you know it would take a person fifteen years to do arithmetic problems that a computer can do in just one second?" he asked. "And computers never make mistakes the way people do. Isn't that amazing?"

"Mmm," said Consuela. She didn't like the idea of something that couldn't be wrong. No excitement, no suspense. It looked as though this would be a dull story!

At last Luis changed the subject. "I liked that story you wrote for the paper last week," he said. "Only your facts were wrong. Don't you ever look things up to be sure of your facts?"

Consuela prickled with anger. Luis was always so sure of himself! She didn't believe facts were as important as feelings. She liked music and books and art—things that couldn't be measured with facts and figures. But that was something Luis would never understand.

"I hope you get the facts straight when you write the story about computers," Luis went on.

"Listen," Consuela said angrily, "I didn't want to write about computers. I don't care about computers. They may be good with numbers, but they bore me!"

"But they're exciting!" said Luis. "The programmer has to give the information to the computer. Then the computer can do amazing things with it. Computers can't think by themselves, but they sure can work fast with the information we give them!"

"I don't want to hear about it!" Consuela broke in. She was convinced that computers were boring. She knew she wouldn't change her mind.

"Say, I'm sorry," Luis said. "I always seem to say the wrong thing. I guess I'm not very good at putting my feelings into words."

"That's for sure," Consuela thought crossly. "Oh, go talk to your wonderful computer," she snapped. They climbed the concrete steps to the computer center in icy silence.

Luis led Consuela into a large room. People were sitting at tables. They were writing out programs, Luis told her. One end of the room was glassed in. Through the glass, Consuela saw rows of large machines, taller than she was.

"Are those computers?" she asked.

"No," said Luis. "Most of the computer is under the floor where you can't see it. These are machines that give information to the computer and get back answers from the computer."

"Oh," said Consuela. All the shiny metal machines made her feel uneasy. She was sure nothing exciting or interesting could come out of this cold place.

Luis was too full of enthusiasm to notice her dismay. "Remember that list of questions I gave you?" he asked.

Consuela nodded. She had filled out the answers to a lot of questions about

herself—about what her favorite colors and foods and hobbies were.

"Well," Luis said, "I took that information and put it into computer language." He held up some cards with holes in them. "All your answers are on these cards. I also had all the boys in our class answer the same questions. When the cards are fed into the computer, it will tell us which boy you have the most in common with."

Luis gave the cards to a man standing at a window which opened into the glassed-in room.

"This might be fun," Consuela thought. She couldn't help feeling interested as she watched the man feed the cards into a slot in one of the machines.

"How long will it take?" she asked.

"Only a very small part of one second," Luis said proudly. "But it takes time to feed our job into the computer.

The computer is doing jobs for a lot of other people, too. So we'll have to wait a few minutes."

They sat at a table in front of a TV screen. "When our job is done," Luis told her, "our number will show on the screen."

Consuela watched numbers appear and disappear on the screen. How could Luis get so excited about all this? But she had to admit she would like to find out which boy the computer matched her with.

All at once, Luis jumped up and went to the window. He came back holding a wide, white sheet of paper. "Here's your answer," he said.

Consuela reached eagerly for the paper. Her mouth fell open in amazement as she read the printed letters.

"It says Luis Perez!" Then she understood.

"You tricked me!" she cried. "You

know we don't have a thing in common!"

Luis grinned. "That's right," he said. "I wanted to show you that a computer can't do anything more than what the programmer tells it to do. If the programmer gives the wrong information to the computer, he'll get the wrong information back."

"I thought a computer never lied," said Consuela.

"It doesn't," Luis said. "But the programmer can lie or make mistakes. A computer is no better than its programmer."

Consuela was so mad she could hardly speak. "You could have told me that without tricking me," she said. "What a rotten thing to do!"

Luis spoke more softly. "I wanted to show you something else," he said. There was a strange shyness in his voice. "Having things in common isn't the only reason people can like each other."

Consuela glanced at him in surprise. He looked anxious, less sure of himself. Was Luis trying to say that he liked her? She felt her anger melt away, and suddenly she began to laugh. What a crazy way to tell a girl you like her! A print-out from a computer!

Luis stared at her for a startled moment, and then he began to laugh with her. "Guess what I told the computer my favorite hobby was," he gasped between bursts of laughter. "Reading poetry!"

Consuela laughed harder. How it must have pained him to write that. But what a lot of work he had gone to for her!

She wiped tears of laughter from her eyes.

"I think I'd like to learn more about computers," she said.

She glanced at the big machines beyond the glass wall. They no longer seemed so boring. This story just might be the best she'd ever written!

ACTIVITY 1

Fact Questions

1. What was Consuela doing when Luis arrived?

2. What work did Luis do in his spare time?

3. Why was Consuela talking to Luis about computers?

4. Where was the computer kept?

5. What kinds of questions were on the list that Luis gave Consuela?

6. Who else answered the questions on Luis' list?

7. What did Luis do with the cards with holes in them?

8. About how long did it take the computer to do Luis' job?

9. What was the name of the boy with whom the computer matched Consuela?

10. Why did the computer give this answer?

2 ACTIVITY — Thought Questions

1. Why did Consuela think that she and Luis were as opposite as two people could be?

2. How did Consuela feel about a machine that never makes a mistake?

3. How did Luis feel about Consuela's not getting facts straight?

4. Why did Consuela think that computers were boring?

5. Why did Luis say he played his trick on Consuela?

6. What other reason might Luis have had for playing that trick?

7. Do you think the trick was fair?

8. Did the machine make a mistake?

9. How had Consuela changed at the end of the story?

10. Was the change in Consuela good or bad? Explain.

3 ACTIVITY

Select the phrase that best completes the statement. Write the number of the statement and the letter of the phrase that best completes it on your paper.

1. The main character in this story is
   a. Consuela.
   b. Luis.
   c. the computer.

2. The plot is the series of events of
   a. a day in class.
   b. an experience of putting a job through the computer.
   c. Consuela's writing a story for the school paper.

3. The setting is a time and place in
   a. the present.
   b. the past before this century.
   c. another planet.

4. The conflict is between
   a. Consuela and the rest of the world.
   b. Luis and the computer.
   c. Consuela who likes feelings and Luis who likes facts.

5. The theme is
   a. Consuela's dislike of machines and her discovery that machines are tools for human purposes.
   b. Consuela's trip to the computer center was a mistake.
   c. Consuela and Luis discover that they are much alike.

When reading in social studies, it is sometimes helpful to change headings into questions. After you have framed a question, you then read to answer that question. You may do that with the next story.

As you read a heading, stop long enough to change it into a question. For example, the first heading, **Arriving at the Right Moment**, could be changed into a question this way: "How did computers arrive at the right moment?" Another question could be "Why did computers arrive at the right moment?" Then as you continue reading, try to find answers to your question. Sometimes an answer will have several parts. For instance, **Computer-Caused Problems** will tell you about several problems caused by computers.

After you have read the story this way, Activity 1 will be easier for you.

All of us will have some kind of contact with a computer, even though we may never work with one, as Luis Perez did, or enter a computer center. You may have come up against a computer without realizing it. Have you made out a magazine subscription? Returned something to a store for credit on a charge account? Licensed a dog? Taken a plane trip?

Computers are entering into our lives more and more. We scarcely notice, now, when a computer takes over a new job. But along with relieving us of some work, our new mechanical servants have brought us some new problems. Read on to find out what these problems are.

The Computer— An Unbottled Genie

Written for this book by Joseph Dempsey.

You remember the story about Aladdin and his lamp. When he rubbed his lamp, a genie appeared. Aladdin was terrified. The genie was ugly and very strong. He had magical powers. Aladdin would have run away in a panic, but it turned out that the genie was his servant. The genie would do everything Aladdin said. In the end, the genie was a big help to Aladdin. But Aladdin never got over being afraid of the genie.

We feel much the same way about

computers. When computers were invented, it was like unbottling a great power. Computers have done an enormous amount of work for us. They will probably do a great deal more in the future. Most people are pleased to have this great power — so long as we are in control.

Arriving at the Right Moment

In a way, computers came along just at the right moment. Cities were growing larger and spreading farther. Along with the megalopolis came many kinds of snarls and tangles. Governors, mayors, city planners, firemen, policemen, air controllers at airports, doctors, nurses, teachers, bankers, and hundreds of others all make the megalopolis go. They all feel the strain of bigness. They can't keep up with all the things that are happening. They can't gather facts fast enough to make needed decisions.

This lack of needed facts has been called an "information lag." It is the time difference between when a decision must be made and when there is enough information to make it. But just when the information lag was becoming a serious problem — along came the computer.

What the Computer Does

The computer, developed over the past twenty-five years, has done much to cut down this information lag. It helps the decision-makers to keep up with what's happening in the megalopolis. The computer can give them needed information almost as soon as a problem arises.

For instance, a computer can predict a pile-up on a factory assembly line. By going quickly to the cause, managers can keep work flowing smoothly. Computers can check bank accounts and send out bills. They can forecast weather, guide airplanes and trains, and direct missiles and space shots. They can even help learning go faster in school.

The computer can help solve the problem of bigness. But remember, the computer is a very powerful servant. We must learn to use it carefully. For the computer, like Aladdin's genie, can cause more problems than it solves. Like so many things we have designed, it can be misused.

What the Computer Is

With all its complex parts and flashing lights, the computer is still just a machine made by humans to serve humans. It can store information fed into it. It has a "memory" that recalls information. It has a "sorter" that, when programmed, can separate different kinds of information. It can solve in a fraction of a second a problem that a team of mathematicians would take years to solve.

The computer is like a brain. Its memory is perhaps better than the human brain. It can give information faster than a person can. But it is still a machine. It can do only what a human tells it to do.

A computer cannot use information until it is programmed. The program directs it how to use the information. A person gives these directions. A computer cannot handle unprogrammed information. It cannot understand ordinary human problems.

Computer-Caused Problems

Suppose that your neighbor is rushing to the hospital with a seriously hurt child. The driver exceeds the speed limit and gets to the hospital just in time. In his mail the next day is a computer-printed summons for a speeding violation.

If a policeman had stopped him on the highway, he would have understood the problem. He probably would have escorted the car to the hospital. The policeman can handle new information without a program. The computer cannot.

Because computers can handle only certain kinds of information in certain ways, some people have had very funny problems. One woman tried to return a sleeping bag to a department store. But every time she returned the package, the computer sent back double the order. When she complained to

the store, they said the computer never made a mistake. When the woman had 32 sleeping bags, she gave up. She didn't have room for 64 sleeping bags.

Mastering the Machine

Computers can do much to solve the problem of bigness. Computers can also be a problem in themselves. Like the automobile, like drugs, like atomic energy, the computer is a good servant if it has a good master. The computer must be used wisely and carefully.

How can we be good masters? Probably by being good human beings. That would mean having feelings for others. It would mean taking time to listen, help, explain, or try to understand a situation. It would mean using one's common sense. It would mean taking responsibility. With people like this in control of it, the computer can be a good servant.

ACTIVITY 1

Write the questions which you made from each of the headings, numbering them in sequence. Each matches one of the statements below. Choose the statement that best answers your question. Write the letter of the statement after your question. The first one is done for you as an example:

1. Why (or how) did computers arrive just at the right moment? C.

A. Computers provide more information faster to solve many problems of bigness and complexity in business and government.

B. The computer is a machine with a "memory" to store information and a "sorter" to separate different kinds of information.

C. Computers arrived just at the time when growing cities had caused an information lag, slowing the ability of authorities to make decisions.

D. We can master the machine by using it wisely and carefully, by being good human beings.

E. A computer will not break a rule to rush a child to the hospital, cannot handle new information without a program, and will repeat a wrong decision over and over.

ACTIVITY 2

The last story compared a computer with a genie. The comparison was mostly for fun. However, it sometimes helps us to remember facts when we compare them with something fanciful like a genie. In Column I are some statements about a genie. In Column II are statements about computers. Find the letter of the statement in Column II which most closely matches the numbered statement in Column I. Clue: The answer to #1 is D.

I	II
1. A genie is powerful.	**A.** Computers can do only what they are told, or programmed, to do by a person.
2. A genie appears ugly and unfriendly.	**B.** Some people fear that computers may not be used wisely.
3. A genie obeys its master.	**C.** Many people, such as factory managers, tax accountants, weather forecasters, etc., are grateful for computers.
4. A master is glad to have a genie's help.	**D.** Computers handle much more information faster than we can.
5. A master is a little afraid of a genie.	**E.** Computers are inhuman machines which have no feelings.

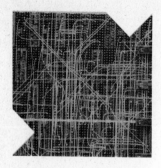

In reading science, we often have to understand *how* things work. We often have to learn a new vocabulary, too. A new idea often brings new words into a language, or new meanings of old words.

This happened when computers were developed. New words and new meanings for old words were added to the language. The description of how computers work is in these new words.

In the next reading, watch carefully for the new words and their definitions. The meaning of a new word is usually nearby, or it may be at the bottom of the page. Do not try to rush through this reading. Go slowly enough to understand each point before you move on to the next point. You may have to read the selection more than once.

Do you think Luis Perez liked computers partly because he would have liked to think that fast himself? How about you? Imagine solving all your math problems in less than a second. You would never need an eraser. You could be a chess expert, guide a rocket, forecast the weather.

A computer makes all those things easier. Let's look a little more closely at what a computer *is*.

Want to Be a Computer?

Written for this book
by Leonard Bernstein.

calculator (kal′kyoo lā′tẽr), person or machine that does addition, subtraction, multiplication, and division

abacus (ab′ə kəs), a frame with beads sliding on wires for doing arithmetic

vacuum (vak′ū əm), empty space. A vacuum tube contains very little air or gas

transistor (tran zis′tẽr), tiny device which controls the flow of current

circuit (sũr′kit), a path over which electric current may flow

binary (bī′nə rē), a set of two

Some scientists think that early men and women wrote numbers even before they wrote words. The numbers were probably records of crops, and animals. Sticks and pebbles might have been used first, and later scratches on the walls of caves. But how many scratches can you make without running out of wall space?

There had to be a better way, and someone found it. The earliest of all calculators was developed more than

2,000 years ago. It was nothing like the calculators we see advertised today. It probably cost a lot less, too. But, if the problems are of a simple kind, it gives answers. It often uses beads strung along a wire. It is called an abacus.

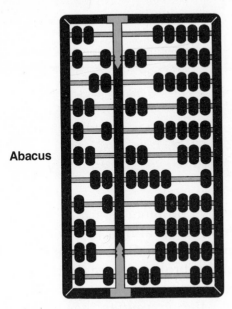

Abacus

In 1642, an arithmetic machine was developed. Numbers were dialed into the machine the way you dial a number on a telephone. The arithmetic machine was followed thirty years later by a calculating machine. As science and mathematics advanced, newer and faster machines were needed. By 1944, the first automatic calculator was being used. It was called the Mark I, and it weighed five tons. It contained more than 500 miles of wire and over 3,000 electrical parts.

Modern computers are no longer the size of a large room. Some are so small that they can be held in one hand. The large vacuum tubes of the early computers were replaced by tiny transistors. These transistors are now being replaced by even smaller electrical parts called block crystals.

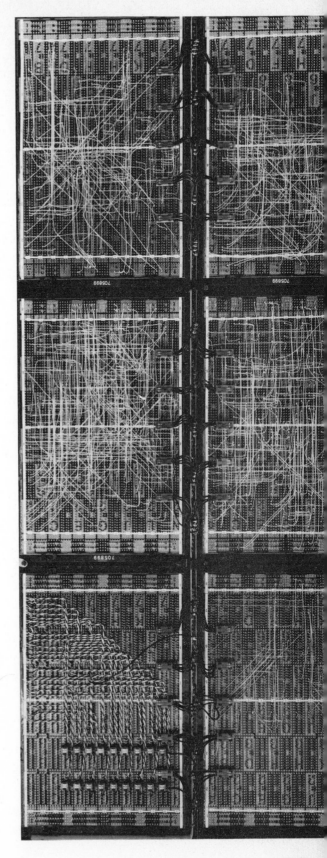

Block crystals contain no wires. A single crystal can replace a dozen vacuum tubes and yards of wire. Groups of block crystals are put together to form complete circuits. Each of these circuits is so small that a microscope must be used to see it.

As the size of a computer decreases, so does the time it takes to solve a problem. While you are reading this sentence, a computer can do more than 15,000 multiplication problems. Amazing but true.

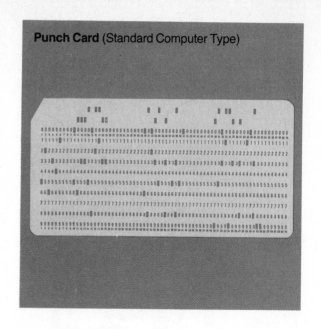

Punch Card (Standard Computer Type)

Computer Language

Computers have a language all their own. This language is very exact and very simple, once you understand it. It is the language of mathematics. Computers respond to electrical signals. To give these electrical signals a meaning, we use a code. This code is called the binary system of numbers. It is the computer's language.

Binary numbers are combinations of just two numbers, 1 and 0. *The number 1 stands for a signal. The 0 stands for no signal.* Any information for the computer must be translated into this code. It is then punched on cards which are fed into the computer. A punched hole represents the number 1. A blank space with no hole is 0. Electrical signals pass through the holes. Where there is no hole, there will be no signal. In this way, the computer receives the information on the card.

How Computers "Think"

Computers don't have a mind of their own. But they do have something like a mind. It is called a problem board. A problem board is filled with wires which allow the computer to solve a problem. Each step of a problem must be broken down into the computer's language. When this has been done, the computer has been programmed. This means that it has the information it needs to solve a problem. The first step in a computer's problem-solving is the *input,* or the feeding of information into the machine. Input is stored in the computer's memory. The second step is the calling back of certain parts of the input from storage in the memory. During the third step, processing, the computer solves the problem.

The answer to the problem is the computer's *output,* which is the final step. A computer's output may be in the form of punched cards, tapes, or sheets of typewritten paper. This answer is in the same code that was used to feed the problem into the machine. A human being then reads it, decodes it, and tells the rest of us the solution to the problem.

194

ACTIVITY 1

1. What is the name of the earliest calculator?

2. About how long ago was the abacus developed?

3. What happened to the large vacuum tubes of early computers?

4. What have transistors been replaced by?

5. During the last thirty years, what has happened to the size of computers?

6. What is the language of the computer?

7. What gives meaning to the electrical signals?

8. What are binary numbers made up of?

9. What is the mind of the computer?

10. When has a computer been programmed?

11. What is input?

12. Where is input stored?

13. What happens during processing?

ACTIVITY 2

1. Why are today's computers smaller than those of 30 years ago?

2. Why does a computer have a language all its own?

3. Why do punch cards sometimes have a warning telling you not to damage the card?

4. Which step in computer problem-solving corresponds to a student memorizing the multiplication table?

5. Which step in computer problem-solving corresponds to a student writing answers on a weekly quiz?

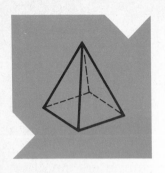

HOW TO READ IN MATHEMATICS

Many of the shapes used in geometry look new and strange when we see them in a mathematics textbook. Yet they are all familiar shapes we have seen before. In the next reading, we will work with the geometric forms of familiar objects.

Computers may seem very strange to us until they are explained. Then we find that many of the elements in the working of a computer are familiar. We know something about electricity, about number systems, about codes. All these familiar things are used in new ways in computers. Read on for familiar things used in new ways in geometry.

Recognizing Geometric Forms

Written for this book
by William L. Schaaf.

On this page there is a column with pictures of real objects and a column with pictures of geometric forms. On your paper, write the names of the real objects and number them. After each, write the name of the geometric form that is most like it. For example, the first real object is a tent. The geometric form most like it is *pyramid*. On your paper you will write: 1. tent—pyramid

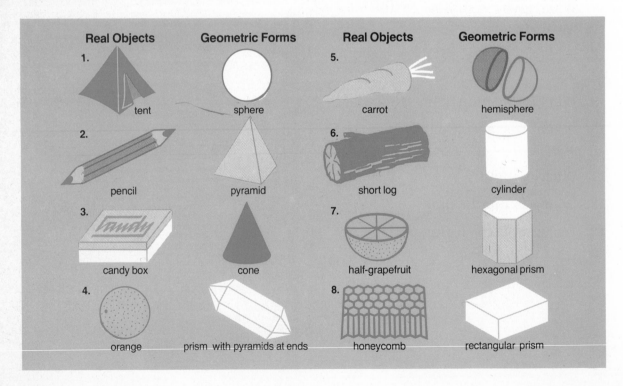

Real Objects	Geometric Forms	Real Objects	Geometric Forms
1. tent	sphere	5. carrot	hemisphere
2. pencil	pyramid	6. short log	cylinder
3. candy box	cone	7. half-grapefruit	hexagonal prism
4. orange	prism with pyramids at ends	8. honeycomb	rectangular prism

ACTIVITY 1

On your paper, write the names of the geometric forms which you recognize in each of these houses or structures. Some will have more than one.

1. Eskimo igloo

2. bank

3. circus tent

4. Indian tepee

5. church steeple

6. gas tank

7. silo

8. South Sea Islander's home

9. water tank

Critical Reading: Facts and Opinions

Students should develop the habit of questioning what they read. Not everything that is in print is accurate. You must decide for yourself whether what is said is a fact, an opinion, or a false idea. Often you will need to look up more information before deciding whether or not the statement is accurate.

There are some clues, however, that are helpful to you. For one thing, look for numbers. If numbers are given, they usually indicate that a survey has been made.

Another clue is that of names and dates. If an article gives the real names of people and places and the exact dates of happenings, you usually can rely on it. Another advantage is that you can check it more easily.

If neither numbers, names, nor dates are given, the information is usually someone's opinion. If the article deals with a subject in science, look to see if a group of scientists agree on this opinion. If the article is in social studies, mathematics, or another special field, try to find out if it was written by a specialist in this subject.

Sometimes you can check on the accuracy of an article by recalling a similar experience. This experience may be one that you or that someone you know has had.

In all cases in which you are in doubt, search for further information. This can be done by referring to encyclopedias and to recent books on the topic in question. Sometimes you may wish to write to an author or publisher to find the source of information given.

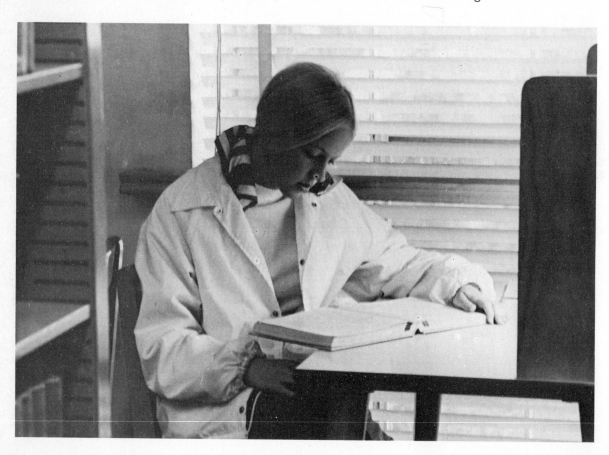

Paragraphs for Critical Reading

Read each of the separate statements or paragraphs below. Write your answers to the questions that follow it on your own paper.

1. This is an old saying: "If you hold a conch shell to your ear, you can hear the ocean roar."

Do you believe that this saying is a fact? Give your own reason as to why or why not.

2. In recent years scientists have become aware of huge fiery objects in the sky. These objects are as massive as a million stars. They have a brightness a hundred times greater than our galaxy of 100 billion stars. Scientists all over the world are trying to find out more information about these objects.

Do you believe that these objects exist in the sky? If so, how can you find out more information about them?

3. Americans eat far more ice cream than do any other people. They eat an average of 23 quarts per person per year. Canada is next. Its people eat an average of 13.5 quarts per person per year. Australians are next. They eat an average of 12.5 quarts per year. No country in Europe comes close to these figures.

Do you think these statements are facts, opinions? Why? How could you find out if the statements are facts?

4. Scientists have found that Mars has seasons in which the color of its surface changes. They say this is proof of life on Mars.

Do the above statements prove to you that there is life on Mars? If not, where would you look to find the best opinion on this subject?

5. There is such a thing as "bait" advertising. The advertiser states that he is selling an article at a greatly reduced price. When you go to buy the article, you are told that it is sold out or that they don't have it in your size. The advertiser thinks that if he gets you into his store, you will buy something else.

Do you believe that "bait" advertising exists? Why? Have you or anyone you know had an experience in "bait" advertising? If so, what was it? Would you need to know about several such experiences before you decided that "bait" advertising exists?

6. Mrs. Holbrook has just moved from the large house in which she lived. This was because of a ghost. One night the ghost banged doors and sent papers and small objects flying all around the house.

Do you believe that there was a ghost in Mrs. Holbrook's house? If so, why? If not, what explanation could you give for papers and small objects flying around the house?

Organizing Information

Two paragraphs are mixed up below. The topic of one is "Playing Football with Computers." The topic of the other is "Computer Art."

Identify the sentences below that belong to "Playing Football with Computers" with a *Pl* after the number of the sentence on your paper. Identify the sentences that belong to "Computer Art" by writing *Co* after the number on your paper.

1. All the information about the teams that are to play is fed into the computer.

2. The computer artist must plan his work and think in a very clear way.

3. Artists can program computers to produce pictures.

4. At the end of the 1970-1971 season, the computer had predicted 43 games correctly and only 22 incorrectly.

5. The computer goes through this information to find the most likely result of the game.

6. A computer produces pictures with more careful detail than is possible by hand.

7. A computer is being used to "play" football before a real game is played on the field.

8. He must direct the computer to draw the lines and curves and shapes he wants.

▪ Finding the Main Ideas and Writing Paragraphs

Answer these questions on a separate sheet of paper.

1. Which sentence do you think might give the main idea in a paragraph titled "Playing Football with Computers"?

2. Which might give the main idea in a paragraph titled "Computer Art"?

3. Now write a well-organized paragraph using all of the sentences about playing football with computers. Be sure to give your paragraph a title.

4. Do the same thing with the sentences about computer art.

How to Find Things in a Library

Libraries are rich storehouses of books in which you can find information about any subject. Your textbooks do not contain all of the information that you need in your study. You can, however, find more information in a library about any topic that you are studying.

Perhaps you have a library in your school. If not, you probably live in or near a city or town that has a library. In either case, go to the library often for information and for pleasure.

You will enjoy your library work more if you can find what you want quickly and easily. On this page you will have practice in using a card catalog. This is one of the most important library skills.

◢ Using a Card Catalog

Every library has cases filled with drawers. These drawers contain cards with names of authors, books, and topics on them. All of these drawers taken together make up what is called a *card catalog*. These cards can be thought of as a huge catalog of everything that is on the shelves of the library.

This is a drawing of the front of a library card catalog. The letters on the drawers are to guide you in finding what you want. If you wanted to look up a topic such as *Africa*, you would look in the drawer marked *A*. If you

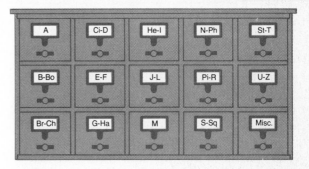

wanted to look up *Hawaii*, you would look in the drawer marked *G-Ha*.

When looking for information about a person, look for the first letter in his or her *last* name. If you wanted to find information about *Louis Pasteur* you would look for *Pasteur* in the drawer marked *N-Ph*.

Complete the rhyme below by filling in the blanks. On your own paper, after the number of each line with a blank, write the letter or letters of the drawer where the topic named will be found.

1. If you want to know about *India*, Drawer ＿＿ has what you're looking for.
2. If you're interested in *coconuts*, ＿＿ is your drawer.

3. Are you learning about *papayas*? Drawer ＿＿ is the place to begin.
4. Want to know about *volcanoes*? ＿＿ is the drawer to look in.

5. Drawer ＿＿ will help you if you're planning a trip to *France*.
6. Try looking in Drawer ＿＿ to learn about the *dance*.

7. The *Carolina Islands* will be found in Drawer ＿＿.
8. To find out about *tornadoes*, look in Drawer ＿＿.

9. Look in Drawer ＿＿ to find out if *ostriches* can fly.
10. When was *Hans Christian Andersen* born? Drawer ＿＿ is the place to try.

Words May Have Different Meanings in Different Subjects

Some words may mean one thing in a certain subject field and something else in another subject field. You will find words of this type in the lists below.

cell	yarn	power	pupil
band	yard	change	cone

Read the first definition. Choose a word from the list that goes with that definition. Write it on your paper. Do the rest of the page in the same way. Each word is used twice.

1. In *mathematics*: a measure which is 36 inches in length

2. In *social studies*: a piece of enclosed ground for some business or other purpose

3. In *social studies*: several persons or animals joined together or working or acting together

4. In *social studies*: a small room in a prison

5. In *science*: a small unit of living matter

6. In *music*: a group of musicians playing instruments together

7. In *science*: the part of evergreen trees that bears seeds

8. In *mathematics*: coins left after making a purchase

9. In *mathematics*: a solid that has a flat, round base and narrows to a point at the top

10. In *social studies*: a thread used in weaving or knitting

11. In *social studies*: places or conditions that become different as time passes

12. In *literature*: a tale

13. In *science* or *health*: a part of the eye

14. In *science*: energy or force that has the ability to do work

15. In *social studies*: one who is learning in school

16. In *social studies*: a person or group which has authority, right, or control over others

Working with Science Words

The words below are used in many science textbooks. You will be able to read better in your science books if you can pronounce all of these words correctly and understand their meanings as they are used in science.

Study the pronunciation of each word. Say the word to yourself. Then read and think about the meaning of the word.

---

barometer (bə rom′ə tẽr), an instrument for measuring air pressure

front (frunt), the leading edge or boundary of an air mass

hydrosphere (hī′drə sfẽr), the part of the earth that is liquid; liquid water on the surface, in the air, and under the ground

luminous (lo͞o′mə nəs), used to describe a body that gives off light

payload (pā′lōd′), whatever a rocket carries

precipitation (pri sip′ə tā′shən), rain, hail, or snow that falls from the sky

thermostat (thũr′mə stat), a device for regulating temperature

thrust (thrust), the force with which an airplane or rocket moves forward

toxin (tok′sin), a poison produced by plants, animals, or germs

vacuum (vak′ū əm), a space from which air or other matter has been removed

---

See if you know the meaning of each of these words as it is used in science. Choose the word that fits the sentence best, adding s if necessary. On your own paper, write the word after the number of the sentence.

1. Usually, the first rockets sent to a body in outer space carry with them a _____ of instruments.

2. Mrs. Stone liked her house comfortable. She set the _____ at 70°F.

3. The Pacific Ocean is a part of the earth's _____.

4. Some food poisoning is produced by _____ from bacteria that grow in food.

5. A great deal of rain fell in Paris last year. The weatherman said that the _____ was very heavy.

6. To test weightlessness, an astronaut goes into a room from which all the air has been removed. The inside of this room is a _____.

7. The weatherman knew that a cold air mass was coming. He said we would soon feel a cold _____.

8. The sun is a _____ body.

9. The weatherman can tell whether the air pressure is going up or down by looking at the _____.

10. The rocket started off with a strong _____.

Working with Social Studies Words _____

The words below appear in widely used social studies, history, and geography books. You will understand your lessons in these subjects better if you know the meaning and pronunciation of these words. Perhaps you think that you can already pronounce each one correctly and that you know the special meaning of each word as it is used in these subjects. Check with the pronunciations and meanings below to be sure.

Study the pronunciation of each word. Say the word to yourself. Then read and think about its meaning.

---

aggression (ə gresh'ən), an attack by one country on another country

ally (al'ī), a person or state united with another for some special purpose

atlas (at'ləs), a book of maps

convict (kon'vikt), a person serving a prison term for a crime

document (dok'yoo mənt), a formal written or printed paper giving information

immigrants (im'ə grənts), people who come to a country or region to live

insurgent (in sũr'jent), a person who rebels or rises against authority

marine (mə rēn'), having to do with the sea

neutral (noo'trəl), on neither side in a quarrel or in war

parliament (pär'lə mənt), the highest lawmaking body of a country

---

See how well you understand the meaning of each of the words above as it is used in social studies. Select the word that fits the sentence best. You may have to add s to some of them. On your own paper, write the word after the number of the sentence.

1. The Constitution of the United States is an important _____.

2. Tom Stevens joined one branch of the Navy for war service at sea. He is a _____.

3. Mary didn't know where India was. So she looked it up in an _____.

4. A group of _____ in prison were taken out to work on the road.

5. A group of _____ in Ireland rebelled against the government of Great Britain.

6. When the Franks invaded Gaul they were guilty of _____.

7. In the United States we have many _____ from Europe.

8. France was an _____ of the colonists in the Revolutionary War.

9. The laws of Great Britain are made by its _____.

10. For many years India hasn't taken sides in any disputes between other nations of the world. This country has been _____.

204